Welfare Management
in Transition
Lessons for Emerging Economies

Welfare Management in Transition

Lessons for Emerging Economies

Editors

N.U. Khan and Sigamani P.

B L O O M S B U R Y

NEW DELHI • LONDON • OXFORD • NEW YORK • SYDNEY

BLOOMSBURY PUBLISHING INDIA PVT. LTD.
London   New Delhi   New York   Sydney

ISBN: 978-93-82563-55-6

Published by Bloomsbury Publishing India Pvt. Ltd.
Vishrut Building, DDA Complex, Building No. 3,
Pocket C-6 & 7, Vasant Kunj
New Delhi 110 070

Laser Typeset by Fortune Graphics
WZ-911/2, Shankarlal Street, Ring Road, Naraina, New Delhi

Printed at Replika Press Pvt. Ltd.

Contents

Preface

This book is a collection of essays, which broadly explore paradigm shifts in social welfare management and recommends lessons for emerging economies, particularly India. We would like to thank scholars who participated in the '*International Conference on Relevance of Policy Reforms on Development: Challenges before Emerging Economies*' and particularly those who contributed articles. We wish to thank the organizations and our sponsors, particularly the University Grants Commission, Jamia Millia Islamia, Indian Council for Medical Research, Powergrid Corporation of India, Maruti Suzuki for their unconditional financial support and assistance. We would like to thank all our colleagues, research scholars, students for their support. Thanks are due to Bloomsbury Publishing India for their efforts in bringing out this book.

N.U. Khan and Sigamani P.

Introduction

N.U. Khan and P. Sigamani

Department of Social Work, Faculty of Social Sciences
Jamia Millia University, New Delhi

There are a broad array of roles and functions that social welfare managers perform, such as addressing management issues and challenges that occur in several fields such as healthcare, family, children's services, services to the aged, water distribution management, provision of basic needs etc. Keeping in mind the multidimensional treatment of social welfare management, this book focuses on the changing welfare management practices and lessons for emerging economies, particularly concerns of equity and inclusive development.

Human services refer to a wide spectrum of organizations in healthcare, educational and social services fields that are presumed to share certain fundamental similarities. Although the settings in which these services are delivered vary widely, these are considered to share a number of similar characteristics that collectively distinguish them from other types of organizations. These include heavy reliance on third party financing, the goal of changing clients, the use of technologies that are not highly determinate, and reliance on the judgement and discretion of front line professional personnel (Austin 1997). In this formulation, the issues confronting managers in these settings are sufficiently similar, to justify a generic model of management (Austin, 2003).

Social welfare management typically refers to management that is shaped by the objectives, technologies and professional cultures found in organizations that deliver personal or social services. This approach has largely focused on public and non profit delivery systems for social services, provided outside the market place (Patti 1983, Rapp & Poertner, 1992 and; Skidmore, 1990). Organizations in social welfare tend to have somewhat less supportive environments, weaker technology and greater resilience on frontline personnel.

Traditionally, in the emerging economies, the social welfare management is dictated by the ideological vent of that state. In a socialist state, social welfare management is largely the state's responsibility. Therefore, agencies of social welfare management are run like governmental bureaucracies. In a capitalist economy with no or minuscule social security, welfare administration emanating from correctional/judicial needs stay with the state while, largely the state's role is residual and social welfare management is done by voluntary organizations. In a mixed economy like India, the role of social welfare management has got distributed among government organizations and non-profit organizations, with a superstructure of foreign international NGOs acting as the main donors, driven by their different objectives.

However, over the last three decades, several industrial democracies and social policy developments have produced a very different kind of clientele for social agencies. One development is the growing disparity of wealth, abetted by economic and tax policies that favor higher income groups. In this context, the rate of poverty, most notably among children, has slowly but steadily risen. Concurrently, there has been rapid growth in the number of older people, with their attendant health and social problems; marked increase in inequality and disparity. Taken together, these trends have converged to produce a broad segment of the population dependent on publicly supported social services. The emerging economies have a peculiarity i.e. unlike developed economies, it is not just the old and children that need state care, but unemployed youth. These new demands of demography compel that new models of social welfare management be explored than have been traditionally present. Therefore, social welfare needs to move away from the traditional system to new welfare management.

Although social welfare management is maturing as a field of practice, however, its intellectual foundations remain shaky. Social welfare management should embrace and adapt organizational theories which effectively address managerial issues within the social welfare context. There is a need to design and implement sound welfare management systems to maintain and process information about populations, applying for benefits under any program administered by the government, or the state. This would promote efficiency in determination of eligibility for public assistance and care to reduce unauthorized and excessive payments in local districts.

Although adapted from the business sector, it proposes a coherent and specific model of management, that is oriented for the satisfaction of consumer needs, and therefore is quite consonant with the purposes of a social welfare organization. Various mechanisms for welfare delivery in a developing economy like India, can be classified into different categories: set asides, income augmenting, safety nets for the aged and direct provision of basic needs. In a developing economy like India, there are several reasons why welfare programs end up poorly. These reasons are broadly grouped under two headings: (a) structural, and (b) political. The nomenclature is more classificatory than descriptive.

The structural reasons stem in a large part from the fiscal crises of state (i.e. provincial) governments. This has led to the increasing dependence on centrally sponsored schemes. The programs are designed and substantially funded by the central government. However, as mentioned in the state list of the Constitution, programme implementation is at the state level. The multiplicity of centrally sponsored schemes makes it difficult for the local level administrative machinery to monitor and execute the schemes.

Hence, structural weaknesses of the local administration have to be examined by the local public administration, despite the programs being well designed and funded. The Achilles heel of all such programs is in their implementation by local public officials. Some new models like SIFs, PPPs need to be explored. The present book is an attempt to present various issues related to social welfare management in India, and lessons for merging economies. The book contains 11 articles which are divided into 11 chapters.

STRUCTURE OF THE BOOK

Suryanarayana states how important it is to have a clear well defined framework, perspective and understanding of the issues, before finalizing the recommendations for policymaking. The author has urged policymakers to seriously review issues relating to food security. The study talks about the challenges facing policy makers about food security in India. The article mentions different policy options for programs and their targeting, to promote food security in the most cost-effective fashion. The author states that the focus now is on the need for targeting food distribution programs. There are several issues which have been highlighted in the article. These include conceptual and empirical issues, which have received little attention, but which are critical for policy formulation and implementation. A major limitation of policy making for food security in India is, that it is without an integrated perspective on concepts, norms, institutions and empirical facts and realities. This study summarizes some of the major issues relevant for policy making in India.

Meenakshisundaram seeks to review the functioning of PDS, in times of both surplus and scarcity, in the context of its role as a safety net for the poor, and suggests suitable policy reforms to make it more effective. The article highlights salient features of the system, the strengths and weaknesses, as it exists today. The assessment of the PDS indicates that while the relevance of PDS as a safety net to the poor has not diminished, the system has confronted several problems such as: identification errors in targeting the poor; complex administration, high administrative costs; poor accountability and beneficiary participation. A major weakness of the PDS is, that it may not succeed in meeting the needs of the targeted poor to a significant extent, leading to any notable impact on household income, nutrition and food security. This programme which involves huge subsidies, may not be cost effective. The author provides some suggestions and recommendations for policy formulation and states, that even though strong political support is essential to establish and maintain the PDS, good governance seems to hold the key to make it an effective safety net for the poor.

Viswambharan, George and Ahamed in their study stress on the need for an effective and efficient system of agricultural marketing to protect farmers from middlemen. Presence of an organized production and marketing set up is essential for the farmers' empowerment. The authors in the study suggest strategic models for initiating farmer-led self help groups and marketing federations in Kerala and other Indian states, based on SWOT (Strengths, Weakness, Opportunities and Threats) analysis of the present system.

The study especially covered Farmers' Organizations (FOs); SHGs; Farmers' Interest Groups (FIGs); Commodity Interest Groups (CIGs) and Market-led Extension. The study states that the production and market intervention of the Vegetable and Fruit Promotion Council Keralam (VFPCK) through its SHGs, and their farmers' market federations have benefited farmers through increased social interaction, increased bargaining power, better knowledge, skill and attitude, better group market culture, better prices and sustainable profits. The study contributes two inter related alternative marketing models namely, the societal marketing model, and the SHGs-linked farmers' marketing model. The former model highlights the overall empowerment of the farmer producers, and the societal advantages to consumers. The latter market model, highlights the importance of crop producing SHGs getting federated as farmers' markets, with an additional focus on crop diversification, diversification of marketable produce, storage, and post harvest processing establishment of retail outlet chains for graded and standardized farm fresh products targeting premium segments, and exporting.

Upinder Sawhney and Amrita Shergill highlight the wave of economic reforms that unlike at the national level, have not shown much dynamism in the reforms process of states, and local levels of the government. Their focus is on the state of Punjab of the Indian Union, which has not witnessed economic progress, and not shown any considerable effectiveness of the reforms process. The researchers talk about why the state was not able to bring about any major changes for many years and pursued populist policies, leading to a major fiscal crisis and economic deceleration in the state. The study stresses on how the Government of Punjab (GOP) had to finally wake up to the need for certain reforms including fiscal, institutional as well as reforms of the state level public enterprises (SLPEs). The authors through this article, seek to evaluate the extent of reforms in the state in the last two decades, and will looked into its success or otherwise, as well as further needs for economic and governance reforms in Punjab.

Arvind Kumar and Ravi studied the socio-economic conditions of self employed women, to measure the impact of micro finance on the group of these women in India. In the light of the findings of this study, the authors have offered recommendations to improve the function of micro finance for self employed women. The researchers present this study with the fervent hope, that this will draw the attention of the authorities, departments and organizations concerned with micro finance and SEW! on various issues, in respect of the development of women empowerment. Through this study they have found that parameters like area of residence, marital status, caste, education and awareness have a major effect on the socio-economic status of women. The study stresses on the need for proper coordination and cohesive efforts by various agencies viz, government, voluntary organizations, commercial banks etc. to alleviate the socio-economic status of self employed women in India.

Bangia tries to scrutinize the functions of the Panchayati Raj Institutions (PRI) and reviews the history of the Panchayati Raj System, and moves on to the challenges that lie ahead. Some of these challenges include: the Directive Principles of State Policy do not have the force of law and are not justifiable, the wide difference between promise and performance by PRIs, problems of power breakdowns, non-supply of water, non-availability of healthcare services, drainage and sewerage problems, no public conveyance for children for going to school. The author has suggested some recommendations for the sustainable functioning of the PRIs. He suggests responsible utilization of the tax sources to the maximum extent possible would devolve on the PRIs in the states. It would thus give the best guarantee for the strength, as well as the autonomy of the PRIs. Leadership, will power, imaginations and tactfulness of the PRIs would go a long way in strengthening the financial base of such PRIs. Periodical elections to PRIs and a frequent change in leadership for better functioning should be kept in view. The article is incisive of the fact that the democratic process loses all its credibility when there is no accountability.

Rashmi Umesh Arora realizes that financial access is an important input for economic development. This study using World Bank (2007) and CGAP (2009) databases, examines the extent of financial access in South Asian countries. The article focuses on the access dimension of finance, which is being recognised as an important issue in economic development. The researcher has examined financial access of countries within the South Asian region and the reason being, it is fast growing, yet has high levels of poverty and low human capital development. The study uses an multiple indicator and multi-dimensional approach to cover as many dimensions of access as possible, builds a financial access index for the South Asian countries, in order to present a more accurate and comprehensive picture of access to finance. The study clearly states that India ranks highest among all the countries in financial access, followed by Sri Lanka and others in the region.

Ganguly focuses on various issues in the education sector in the Indian scenario. The article gives a detailed account of the various policies framed for improving the condition of the education sector. These include: The policy framework for the development of education, and eradication of illiteracy laid down in the National Policy on Education (NPE)1986, the Universal Declaration of Human Rights, asserting the right to education for all, and Sarva Shiksha Abhiyan launched by the Government of India in 2001. The article focuses on the present state of the education sector in India. Various issues have been highlighted and suggestions made. One of the major goals of universal retention by 2010 has not been achieved so far, and to achieve it, there is need to revamp the programme in a more holistic and comprehensive manner.

Habeebul Rahiman and Hasanul Banna attempts to evaluate the effectiveness of the service delivery of mainstream micro finance institutions by identifying its shortcomings. They also present an interest free cooperative model of micro finance as an alternative, which not only overcomes the shortcomings of the mainstream micro finance system, but also functions as a promising tool for addressing massive poverty and unemployment, boosting human and cooperative feelings among fellow beings in a sustainable manner. According to them, unlike the interest based microfinance systems, which fail to deliver, interest free microfinance institutions and banks prove to be sustainable, and face grave financial crises. The authors urge social workers to explore the potential of this emerging system to answer the present day crisis of the large mass of poor and marginalized people in our country.

Saharey attempts focus on the necessity of a critical examination of the currently ongoing structural educational adjustments and reforms. He attempts to study the extent, and in what ways do the oppressive and unjust hierarchies of the caste system continue to 'lock' Dalit children out of full participation in education within schools. Issues such as status of residential schools for Dalit children, sensitivity of teachers towards Dalit children, infrastructure of schools located in Dalit habitations, scholarships for Dalit children, and quality of education have been highlighted in the study. The author urges state governments to participate rather than withdrawing from social sectors of education and health, and delegating its social commitments and responsibilities to private agencies and non-governmental organizations. He argues that in order for social policy to adequately respond to social exclusion in primary education in India, a holistic approach should be adopted, including addressing the structural and basic causes of the problem in a context-specific, comprehensive manner.

BIBLIOGRAPHY

[1] Austin Michael J. (2003), 'The Changing Relationship between Nonprofit Organizations and Public Social Service Agencies in the Era of Welfare Reform', *Nonprofit and Voluntary Sector Quarterly* 2003 32: 97, accessed on 14th August 2012 at http://nvs.sagepub.com/content/32/1/97.full.pdf+html.

[2] Austin David M., (1997), 'The Institutional Development of Social Work Education: The First 100 Years—And Beyond', *Journal of Social Work Education*, 33 (3): 599-612. Accessed on 14th August 2012 at http://www.jstor.org/stable/pdfplus 23043092.pdf? acceptTC=true

[3] Skidmore Rex Austin (1990), 'Social Work Administration: Dynamic Management and Human Relationships', Michigan, Prentice Hall.

[4] Rapp, C.A. and Poertner J. (1992), 'Social Administration: A Client-Centered Approach', New York, Longman.

[5] Patti, R. (1983), 'Social Welfare Administration: Managing Social Programmes in a Developmental Context', Englewood Cliffs, Prentice Hall.

[6] Carvalho, S. (1994). 'Social Funds Guidelines for Design and Implementation' (HRO Working Paper No. 34). Washington: World Bank.

[7] Freiberg-Strauáss, J. (1995, December), Consultation Paper of the Task Force of the Working Group Composed of Government and Nongovernmental Institutions, Fighting Poverty Through Self-Help.

[8] Khadiagala, L. (1995, January), 'Social Funds: Strengths, Weaknesses, and Conditions for Success', ESP Discussion Paper Series No. 52, Washington: World Bank.

[9] Marc, A. et al. (1995). 'Social Action Programs and Social Funds, A Review of Design and Implementation in Sub-Saharan Africa' (World Bank Discussion Papers, Africa Technical Department Series), Washington: World Bank.

[10] Parish, L. and Kolp, S. (1994, December), 'Guatemala's Social Funds, A Research Report and Guide for Ractitioners', Washington: Center for Democratic Education.

Food Security in India: Policy Challenges

M.H. Suryanarayana

Indira Gandhi Institute of Development Research (IGIDR), Mumbai

ABSTRACT

Policymaking is serious business. It is very important to have a clear well defined framework, perspective and understanding of the issues, before finalizing the recommendations. This is one area, which calls for serious review and reform in India. This article illustrates one such issue relating to food security.

What are the challenges facing policy makers on food security in India? Generally, one hears about hurdles in implementation. Much has also been said about different policy options for programmes and their targeting to promote food security in a most cost-effective fashion. In recent years, the focus has been on the need for targeting food distribution programmes. Expert groups and the Eleventh Plan have even recommended universal targeting. The National Advisory Council on the National Food Security Act, has already prepared a draft on delivery' mechanisms without a concept and norm for food security.

There are several issues, conceptual and empirical, which have received little attention, but which are critical for policy formulation and implementation. A major limitation of policy making for food security in India is, that it is without an integrated perspective on concept, norm, institutions and empirical facts and realities. This note would summarize some of the major issues relevant for policy making in India.

INTRODUCTION

While the Government of India has constituted several expert groups to define and suggest the methodology for estimation of poverty, it is yet to come out with an official definition of, and norm for food security.[1] Even the National Advisory Council on the Food Security Act, does not seem to have addressed the issue pertaining to the concept and norm.

There have been three different types of shifts in approach to the problem of food security: (i) From the global and the national, to the household and the individuall; (ii) From the food-first perspective to a livelihood perspective; and (iii) From objective indicators to subjective perceptions (Maxwell, 1996). Choice of specifications of the approach and emphasis would have a considerable bearing on policies and programmes. However, such issues have received little attention. Nevertheless, they matter, given the fact that one's conclusions on food security in India would differ, depending on the approach and norm used.

Policy decisions on food requirements and estimates of incidence of calorie deficiency (used as a synonym for food insecurity in literature), are made with reference to a norm of 2400 calories, a norm considered by the National Planning Committee of the Indian National Congress in 1938, that is more than half a century back. What is missed out in this analysis is, that with economic growth and development involving structural and technological changes, calorie requirements must have declined, as reflected in the observed consumer behaviour of Indian households since Independence. Hence, it is high time that the government sets up a committee to look into issues relating to minimum calorie norms by age-gender-activity composition in India.

However, academic experts, as well as policy makers, have been looking at issues without a well- defined framework and concept, that too with little appreciation of the observed changes during the development process since Independence. Some relevant questions would be as follows:

1. How significant is the improvement in the economic status of the poor?
2. What are the changes in production conditions and institutions, and their implications for food consumption of the poor?
3. What are their policy implications?

Many studies have attempted to answer these questions quite mechanically, with little appreciation of the data generation process and its implications, in the course of development marked by changing institutions and labour markets.

Almost all the studies are based on the National Sample Survey (**NSS**) data on consumption distribution. The NSS seeks to obtain an unbiased estimate of average

---

[1] For that matter even the latest Expert Group Report on poverty is without a concept and norm (Government of India (GoI), 2009b).

household consumer expenditure, with little emphasis on the distributional parameters. For instance, the NSSO clearly lays down instructions to the field investigators as follows:

> *Cooked meals should consist of cooked meals purchased from the market (hotels, restaurants, canteens, etc.). No entries are required for meals prepared at home and consumed by members or visitors of the household. Meals received by an employee's household as perquisites from an employer's household should be left out of account at the employee's household, because these meals are already accounted for in the employer's household, not in the form of meals, but in terms of their constituent items like cereals, pulses, vegetables, edible oil, salt, etc.* (GoI, 1972: p. 121).

Thus, it includes consumption out of home-grown stock, gifts, loans, etc., but not perquisites like 'cooked meal' in the employer's house.

This kind of emphasis, involves collection of information on only food cooked at home, but not food-consumed from wages-in-kind. Wages-in-kind used to be a major mode of wage payments during the 1950s and 1960s. As a result, food consumption in poor labour households got underestimated, and their food insecurity got overestimated. Its converse profile would be over estimation of food consumption of the rich employer households, as reflected in the NSS estimates of food consumption of the richest decile group in the neighbourhood of a kilo of cereals per capita per day in the 1950s, which if correct, would be a miracle by itself.

An empirical illustration is provided as follows:

- In 1960-61, 37 per cent of the rural poor households belonged to rural labour households (Minnas,1974; p. 261). During the 1950s and 1960s, wage payments in kind (primarily prepared food given by the employer) used to be substantial. As per the Second Agricultural Labour Enquiry, agricultural labourers were paid in-kind wage payments for about 50 per cent of the person-days worked in 1956-57.'

  Consistent with this evidence, the NSS estimates show very low levels of cereal consumption for the bottom decile groups during the 1950s and 1960s. As one would expect, estimates for the richest decile group are very high, in some years as high as 26 kg per capita per month, which is almost a kilogram per capita per day. Thus, there must have been substantial underestimation of food grain consumption, virtually the consumption basket, of the poorer labour class and hence, significant overestimation of poverty for the 1950s and 1960s.

- In 1983, agricultural labour households constituted 30.70 per cent of the total rural households, but accounted for nearly half (45.59 per cent) of the total rural poor households. Other rural labour households accounted for 6.57 per cent of the total rural labour households, and 5.99 per cent of the rural poor households. Incidence of poverty (corresponding to the poverty line of Rs. 76.65 per capita per month) was the highest (45.45 per cent) among the agricultural labour households (Suryanarayana, 1998a;p. 46).

What would be the implications of such a data generation process for temporal estimates of poverty (economic dimension of food insecurity)? This would mean that time series, food security profiles based on the NSS estimates of consumption across decile groups of population would be misleading. A careful interpretation would have to take into account the nature and extent of changes in the labour market, including the mode of payment, which have also changed over time as the following shows.

There has been an increase in casualisation of labour since the mid-seventies (GoI, 1996). This must have meant a progressive reduction in in-kind wage payments, and increasing monetisation of the labour market. This must have been reinforced by the process of marginalisation, that is, increase in the proportion of holdings in the marginal category (size of operated holdings less than 1.01 ha.) since the 1970s must have reinforced such a trend. The proportion of marginal owners increased from 39.1 per cent in 1960-61 to 45.8 percent in 1970-71, and finally to 62.8 per cent in 1991-92. During the same period, the size of the large farmers declined from 4.5 per cent to 3.1 per cent and to 1.3 per cent respectively (GoI,1997; p. 20). In 1983, a rural household distributed only 1.6 number of meals per month to its employees (Minhas, 1991; p. 7). In 1993-94, the proportion of rural households which received some wages or salaries in kind was only 7.1 percent, in the form of food was 6.6 per cent, and in the form of cooked food was a mere 2.1 per cent (GoI, 1998; p. 42).

---

[2] Government of India's (GoI) *Agriculture Labour in India,* Report on the Second Survey, Volume I, All India (p. 107) cited in Jose (1978; p. A-16).

[3] On an average, even for these (7.1 per cent) households, which reported receipt of some wages in kind cooked meals, accounted for only 28.41 per cent of their wage payment in the form of food. It was Rs. 46.73 out of 164.44 per cent reporting households. Wage receipt in the form of cooked meal constituted only 16.62 percent of their total monthly per capita total consumer expenditure (Rs. 281) (GoI, 1998; p. 38). .

Such a reduction in in-kind wage payment should lead to a corresponding decline in (a) the estimates of food grain consumption of the employer households; and (b) the under-recording of food consumption of the labour households. The estimates of cereal consumption by decile groups show a marked decline for the richest decile group from about 26 kg in the 1960s, to about 20 kg in the early 1970s, and finally to 15.5 kg in 1993-94 (Table 1).[4] The observed changes in institutions, market structures and relations would bear the data generating process and hence, estimates of food consumption. One would expect a decline in under-recording of food consumption of the labour households, and a corresponding increase in the monetised part of their consumption, involving increases in cereals and complementary items like milk and milk products, fruits, vegetables, nuts and edible oils, at least to the extent warranted by replenishments for the loss due to reduced payments in-kind. This would be reflected, as found for India, in increase in food security and diversification of the food basket.

One may think that this kinds of anomalies do not exist any longer with casualisation and hence, monetisation of the rural labour market since the 1970s. Nevertheless, the data seems to be plagued with errors of a different kind. This may be illustrated with reference to the data on distribution of eligibility cards for subsidized food from the food distribution programme, called the Public Distribution System (PDS) in India. Table 2 provides a profile of the beneficiaries of subsidized food grains from the PDS for the year 2004-05. The beneficiary households are classified as between poor, that is, those below the poverty line (BPL) and non-poor, that is, those above the poverty line (APL) households. Since December 2001, the Government of India has introduced another category called the *Antyodaya* to provide ten million poorest BPL households with 25 kg of food grains at highly subsidised prices of Rs. 2 per kg for wheat and Rs. 3 per kg for rice. The estimated poverty lines for rural and urban India for the year 2004-05 are Rs. 356.30 and Rs. 568.60 respectively.

The table shows that the majority of the households with *Antyodaya* & Below Poverty Line ration cards are in the non-poor/richer monthly per capita expenditure classes (Table 2). The National Sample Survey Organisation (NSSO) explains this anomaly, by stating that "A poor household that bought a durable good during the 30 days prior to the date of survey might conceivably be placed in a higher MPCE class than the class in which its usual MPCE lies" (GoI 2007, p. 16; Footnote # 3).

A moot question would be how valid is the explanation provided by the NSSO, which comes under the Ministry of Statistics and Programme Implementation? On data verification

---

[4] Estimates show a similar decline in cereal consumption for other decile groups also

Table 1: Monthly Per Capita Total Cereal Consumption (kg.) by Decile Groups: All India Rural

Select NSS Rounds	NSS Survey Period	Decile Group										
		0-10	10-20	20-30	30-40	40-50	50-60	60-70	70-80	80-90	90-100	0-100
4	April-Sept. 1952	8.71	12.51	13.68	15.58	16.75	18.33	19.16	19.82	22.69	25.46	17.27
5	Dec. 1952-March 1953	9.72	12.28	14.30	17.05	18.31	20.20	18.97	22.14	22.93	24.62	18.06
4&5	April 1952-March 1958	9.28	12.39	14.14	16.25	17.85	18.64	19.54	20.59	22.83	24.96	17.64
13	Sept. 1957-May 1958	9.25	12.61	14.29	14.67	15.73	16.79	18.45	19.12	19.96	25.65	16.65
14	July 1958-June 1959	9.08	12.58	13.77	15.39	16.94	17.73	19.16	20.88	21.67	26.10	17.33
15	July 1959-June 1960	10.18	12.62	14.28	15.22	16.89	17.85	18.71	19.61	22.27	26.17	17.38
16	July 1960-Aug. 1961	10.22	12.91	15.01	16.74	17.13	18.36	18.85	18.82	21.55	25.51	17.51
17	Sept. 1961-July 1962	11.42	13.31	14.88	15.64	15.83	17.98	19.11	19.67	21.39	26.28	17.55
27	Oct. 1972-Sept. 1973	9.08	12.03	13.32	14.35	15.15	15.60	17.07	17.75	18.96	21.26	15.46
28	Oct. 1973-June 1974	9.50	12.22	13.30	14.08	15.09	16.16	16.62	17.23	18.52	20.87	15.21
32	July 1977-June 1978	9.72	12.46	13.68	14.27	15.20	15.77	16.51	17.44	18.45	20.48	15.40
38	January-December 1983	10.35	12.45	13.38	13.94	14.78	15.29	15.66	16.34	17.41	19.40	14.90
42	July 1986-June 1987	9.96	12.08	12.90	13.68	14.16	14.73	15.48	15.95	16.57	18.48	14.40
50	July 1993-June 1994	10.53	12.09	12.65	13.22	13.40	13.77	14.12	14.46	14.65	15.52	13.44
55	July 1999-June 2000	10.49	11.65	12.30	12.59	12.92	13.09	13.43	13.54	13.81	14.18	12.80
61	June 2004-July 2005	10.16	11.08	11.44	11.71	11.89	12.11	12.34	12.50	12.45	15.81	12.15

Source: Suryanarayana (2000, 2000a)

in detail, we find that about 75 per cent of such non-poor households with BPL cards, did not spend anything on durables (Suryanarayana, 2009b). If so, what does the data measure and represent? How far one can pursue analysis of food insecurity of the poor? In fact, one finds such anomalies, because the state governments in several states like Kerala and Tamil Nadu have gone about targeting the PDS to a much larger subset of the population than that recommended by the Planning Commission. The NSSO does not seem to be aware of this fact. The Planning Commission too drafts the Eleventh Five Year Plan, and recommends universal PDS, without really showing any awareness of profiles of the kind displayed in Table 2. An Expert Group set up by the Planning Commission to look into the definition and estimation of the poverty line, poverty does not bother to care for this kind of data anomalies, and hence, data suitability for redefining the methodology, even after a background paper has raised such issues.

Table 2: Percentage of A&BPL Households by MPCE Class
and their Reliance on The PDS: 2
All India

Rural Sector				Urban Sector			
MPCE class	*% of A&BPL House- holds*	*% of consumption from PDS by A&BPL House-holds*		*MPCE class*	*% of A&BPL House- holds*	*% of consumption from PDS by A&BPL House- holds*	
		Rice	*Wheat*			*Rice*	*Wheat*
0–235	48.8	30.27	35.84	0–335	33.4	41.94	31.25
235–270	44.3	27.90	28.43	335–395	28.3	38.79	30.61
270–320	40.8	27.97	29.51	395–485	26.4	33.34	32.18
320–365	38.3	26.95	26.44	485–580	19.9	37.04	33.34
365–410	33.9	26.40	30.39	580–675	17.8	35.25	28.67
410–455	33.1	25.51	28.01	675–790	11.6	32.56	22.98
455–510	31.0	27.91	27.99	790–930	10.1	34.28	20.84
510–580	25.7	27.28	27.65	930–1100	6.9	32.35	14.57
580–690	23.8	28.54	29.27	1100–1380	4.1	23.20	22.89
690–890	19.8	28.13	23.90	1380–1880	2.2	26.79	5.22
890–1155	15.2	27.43	18.07	1880–2540	1.5	17.36	8.91
1155 & more	12.0	21.85	24.03	2540 & more	0.9	25.35	30.27
All classes	29.4	27.40	28.16	All classes	11.3	34.95	28.08

Source: Estimates based on GoI (2007).

Note: Percent of A&BPL households = Percentage of households with *Antyodaya* and BPL ration cards in each expenditure class.

POOR APPRECIATION OF METHODOLOGICAL ISSUES

The most important limitation seems to be the limited capacity for appreciating even elementary statistical tools. For instance, the Eleventh Plan documents carries out trend analysis of the levels of living, food and nutritional status of the poor consumption, with reference to per capita measures of corresponding variables, little realizing that mean based estimators of averages are inappropriate for skewed distributions like that of income or consumption. As a result, the Plan ends up making factually wrong inferences, and empirically irrelevant policy recommendations (Suryanarayana, 2009b).

Another major limitation of even expert groups, is the lack of careful appreciation of elementary concepts and measures. For instance, the Expert Group on the Methodology for the BPL Census 2009 does not even distinguish between a household and person (GoI, 2009b). It keeps citing 28.3 as the percentage number of poor persons, as well as households. It cannot be both, since generally, the poorer households are larger. Another limitation of the studies on welfare consequences of policies to promote food security like the public distribution system, is due to inadequate appreciation of contemporary policy interventions in an integrated perspective. For instance, government documents, as well as non government research reports, estimate welfare gains in terms of differentials between market and PDS prices. However, this would not make much sense, since market prices themselves are determined by, inter alia, public interventions like restrictions on inter-state movement of food grains to facilitate food grain procurement for the PDS, in states having food grain surplus. Due to such interventions, food grain prices are suppressed in food grain surplus regions, and escalated in food deficit areas, generating an exaggerated profile of income transfers in the latter. In fact, such calculations overlook an important fact that the PDS supplies meet only a fraction of the food grain requirements of a household and hence, ignore welfare loss due to escalation in food grain prices in the open market, which meets the bulk of the food requirements of the average household.

Several studies have attempted to examine welfare consequences of public interventions to promote food security, in terms of a consumer demand model, specified and estimated based on the aggregate sample data for the country as a whole. One is not sure how valid such a specification would be. This is because the all-India sample is obtained by a simple pool of sample observations across states. While statistically it would make sense as an average household, conceptually one would doubt the existence of a representative consumer, with an utility function implied by the statistical average. Even otherwise, the procedure would be valid if only the economic constraint binding the households across states is the same, and the preferences are linear and additive, which are highly unrealistic.

PURSUIT OF ECONOMIC REFORMS

The economic reforms era in India has been initiated with much promise. A major programme agenda has been to promote food security at least cost. In pursuit of this goal, several suggestions have been made to reform the public distribution system (PDS), which had cost the public exchequer quite heavily in terms of the food subsidy (Geetha and Suryanarayana, 1993).[5] The policy proposals suggested and considered to reduce the food

---

[5] Budget estimate of food subsidy (proceeds from PDS sales minus costs of procurement, buffer stocks and incidental expenses) for 1992-93 was Rs 2800 crore which amounted to 39 per cent of the total budget deficit (see Geetha and Suryanarayana, ibid.)

subsidy and hence, the budget and the fiscal deficit are quite diverse, but have severe limitations.[6] Unfortunately, these proposals are made without, clear definition of concepts and issues. A few studies have shown that some of these proposals are quite unrealistic.[7] For instance, the proposal on targeting in its original formulation did not really bother about Type I error in targeting[8]; a policy package for minimizing Type I and Type II errors, but subject to some nutrition norms would not have saved but cost the government several folds (Geetha and Suryanarayana, 1993). The proposal to change the commodity composition of the PDS is based on the faulty perception that the poor's food (cereal) basket consists largely of coarse cereals. While this used to be true in the 1950s, it is no longer so. The consumption baskets of the poor have undergone changes, in favour of superior cereals, due to a variety of reasons like changes in tastes, preferences, income and availability. In rural India, coarse cereal consumption is equi-proportionate across decile groups (Suryanarayana, 1995b).

Similarly, the recommendation for food stamps does not really bother to examine the empirical constraints like an efficient market infrastructure to ensure physical access to food (Suryanarayana, 1995c). Most importantly, some of the cost and benefit analyses are made in terms of estimates of budgetary costs, with benefits by income transfers through the PDS (given by the excess of the open market price over that of the PDS). These kind of estimates on income transfer would make little sense. The PDS meets the households cereal requirements only to a partial extent. Further, open market prices, levels as well as their regional and/or seasonal variations, depend largely upon government policy interventions like procurement, buffer stocks, and restrictions on food grain movement. There is enough empirical evidence to show that the poor households resort to the PDS only when the open market price rises beyond their reach (Suryanarayana, 1995a). In other words, the open market PDS price gap co-varies with the extent of hardship imposed on the poor, and does not measure an income transfer.

Related to this, the Government appointed a high level committee on Long Term Grain Policy (HLCGP) to look into, inter alia, functioning of the targeted PDS and fair price shops and viability of fair price shops (GoI. 2002). The HLCGP challenged the general

---

[6] Some of the proposals suggested arc (i) dismantling the PDS; (ii) target the PDS to the poor by means testing; (iii) change the commodities supplied from superior cereals to coarse cereals; and (iv) replace the PDS by food stamps.

[7] See Dev and Suryanarayana (1991), Geetha and Suryanarayana (1993), Suryanarayana (1995a, 1995b, 1995c & 2009) and Suryanarayana and Silva (2007).

[8] Type I error in a targeted welfare programme refers to its failure to benefit the deserving beneiciaries, say, the poor and Type II error to its failure to exclude the unintended beneficiaries, say, the non-poor (Cornia and Stewart, 1993).

perception that India has achieved food security. The general perception was based on (i) estimated reductions in poverty in India from 51.3 per cent in 1977-78 to 36 per cent in 1993-94 and 26.1 per cent in 1999-2000 (GoI, 2004; p. 204); and (ii) surplus stocks and exports of food grains (GoI, 2004. p. S-21). However, the HLCGP disagreed because it considered surplus stocks of food grains were due to the decline in per capita cereal consumption, rather than increases in food production (GoI, 2002). It defined neither the concept of food security, nor any norm for it. Its estimates showed that more than 70 per cent of the population had a per capita energy intake less than 2100 calories per day for some years since 1993-94. In addition, its findings showed that the bottom 80 per cent of the rural, and the bottom 40 per cent of urban households spent more than 60 per cent of their total expenditures on food. This led the HLCGP to conclude that the magnitude of food insecurity was more than the incidence of poverty in India.

What are the implications of a targeted PDS for a food-insecure India? The HLCGP pointed out that the PDS had been introduced to ensure price stability and food security. However, the targeted PDS introduced in 1997, charged differential prices for the poor and non-poor, such as to restrict subsidies only to the poor. In consequence, PDS off-take and profitability for retail PDS outlets declined, as well as the potential to ensure price stability. Because the price instability increased, the HLCGP concluded that the targeted PDS had imposed a penalty on states with a low incidence of poverty, but with relatively high incidence of calorie deficiency. Therefore it recommended universal PDS (GoI, 2002). This policy recommendation was made without reading the distributional profile, and wrongly using outdated subsistence norms. It is the rich who have reduced their cereal consumption and calorie intake; the poorest decile groups have in fact increased theirs. This issue, therefore, calls for a revision in the subsistence norm, and not a 'universal PDS' (Suryanarayana and Silva, 2007).

The Eleventh Five Year Plan carried the HLCGP analysis on food security a step further (GoI. 2008a). It was also not based on a careful and efficient use of statistical facts and their appreciation. It interpreted, commented and recommended policies on issues concerned with deprivation, with reference to estimates of mean-based averages and not distributional profiles. As simple statistics would tell us, the mean is not a robust estimator

---

[9] Since the Eleventh Plan believed that purchasing power was a serious constraint on household food security, it evaluated the PDS in terms of rupees transferred as given by the difference between average market price and the PDS, price and concluded that what matters is possession of a ration card and its type and not economic status of the household. Finally, it recommended (in terms of averages only) that, given the prevailing inequities in distribution, the average calorie availability in the country should be at 'least 20 per cent higher than the per capita requirement (i.e. 2100 calories for urban and 2400 calories for rural areas)' (GoI, 2008a, p. 132).

of the average for skewed distributions. It largely represents changes in the upper percentiles for the variables under review. This is precisely what we find with the NSS estimates for India. The HLCGP also noted reductions in average per capita cereal consumption and calorie intake for the rural and urban populations, during the past three decades. It observed that average calorie intakes in both rural and urban areas have fallen increasingly short of the calorie norms for official poverty lines for the rural (2400 calories) and urban (2100 calories) India. It explained the decline in average cereal consumption and hence, calorie intake of the population in terms of. *inter alia*, stagnant real incomes. It even stated: "Low and stagnating incomes among the poor has meant that low purchasing power remains a serious constraint to household food and nutritional security, even if food production picks up as a result of interventions in agriculture and creation of total infrastructure" (GoI, 2008a. p. 128). As regards policies, the Plan evaluated the PDS and concluded "the PDS seems to have failed in serving the second objective of *making food grains available to the poor. If it had, the consumption levels of cereals should not have fallen on average* – as it has consistently over the last two decades" (GoI, 2008a; p. 135).

The Plan analysis and recommendations call for a scrutiny given its implications for economic policies and programmes. However, much of it is fancied rather than real. A careful review of changes in consumer expenditures and consumption patterns by decile groups in rural and urban India shows, that real consumption expenditure of all decile groups, the bottom three decile groups in particular, increased since the mid-70s (Suryanarayana, 2009). Contrary to the Eleventh Plan speculation, cereal consumption and hence, calorie intake has increased for the bottom decile groups, and declined only for the upper decile groups. This has led to a decrease in the average estimate and increase in the incidence of calorie deficiency. The decline in calorie intake has happened only for the upper decile groups, which cannot be due to any income constraints. In other words, there is no basis for recommending implicit income transfers, even if it is defined, for the total population by universal PDS, to facilitate an increase in average calorie intake.

CONCLUSION

A sound institutional base for information generation and its use is a prerequisite for efficient and effective economic policies. It also calls for the capacity for appreciation of the data inadequacies and implications of the data generation process in a changing institutional environment, in the context of economic development. Equally important is coordination across different government agencies and institutions, and an integrated perspective. Finally, choice of appropriate statistical measures also matters as much as the data generation process. Otherwise, one would end up making inappropriate policy choices and recommendations. For instance, the Indian Eleventh Plan draws attention to a decline in mean based estimates of average food consumption, and also calorie intake since the 1970s. It interprets these estimates as representing a similar worsening of the food insecurity of the poor, little realizing that mean based estimates are not robust measures of averages for skewed distributions, since they represent changes in upper percentiles, and not those in the poorer ones. Such limitations combined with lack of an integrated perspective and conceptualization of goals for food security and inclusive growth, have only complicated matters in the pursuit of food security. In sum, this evidence makes a sad commentary on the state of policy making for the poor and food insecure in India.

REFERENCES

[1] Geetha, S. and Suryanarayana, M.H. (1993). "Revamping PDS: Some Issues and Implications", *Economic and Political weekly*, Vol. XXVIII, No. 41, pp. 2207-2213.

[2] Government of India (1972). "Appendix III: Extracts from Instructions to Field Workers: NSS Nineteenth Round: July 1964-June 1965" in Tables with Notes on Consumer Expenditure. The National Sample Survey Nineteenth Round: July 1964-June 1965, Report No. 192, National Sample Survey Organisation, New Delhi, pp. 117-124.

[3] Government of India (1997). "A Note on Operational Land Holdings in India" 1991-92. NSS 48h Round (January-December 1992), Sarvekshana, Vol. XX, No. 3, pp. 1-64.

[4] Government of India (1998): "A Note on Wages in Kind, Exchange of Gifts and Expenditure on Ceremonies & Insurance in India, NSS 50th Round (1993-94)", *Sarvekshana*. Vol. XXI, No. 3, pp. 29-49.

[5] Government of India (2002). Report of the High Level Committee on Long-term Grain Policy. Ministry of Consumer Affairs, Food & Public Distribution, New Delhi.

[6] Government of India (2004). Economic Survey 2003-04, Ministry of Finance, New Delhi.

[7] Government of India (2007). Public Distribution System and Other Sources of Household Consumption 2004-2005, Volume I, NSS 61 Round (July 2004-June 2005), National Sample Survey Organisation, Ministry of Statistics and Programme Implementation, New Delhi.

[8] Government of India (2008a). Eleventh Five Year Plan 2007-12, Volume II, Social Sector, Planning Commission. Oxford University Press, New Delhi.

[9] Government of India (2008b). Economic Survey 2007-2008, Ministry of Finance, New Delhi.

[10] Government of India (2009a). Economic Survey: 2009-10, Economic Division, Ministry of Finance, New Delhi.

[11] Government of India (2009b). Report of the Expert Group to review the Methodology for Estimation of Poverty, Planning Commission, New Delhi.

[12] Maxwell, Simon (1996). "'Food Security' a post-modern perspective". *Food Policy*, Vol. 21, No. 2, pp. 155-170.

[13] Minhas, B.S. (1974). "'Rural Poverty', Land Redistribution and Development Strategy: Facts", *Indian Economic Review* reprinted in Srinivasan, T.N. and Bardhan, P.K. (eds.) (1974) op. cit., pp. 252-263.

[14] Minhas, B.S. (1991). "On Estimating the Inadequacy of Energy Intakes: Revealed Food Consumption Behaviour Versus Nutritional Nomis (Nutritional Status of Indian People in 1983)". *The Journal of Development Studies*, Vol. 28, No. 1, pp. 1-38.

[15] Rao, C.H. Hanumanlha (1994). Agricultural Growth, Rural Poverty and Environmental Degradation in India, Oxford University Press, New Delhi.

[16] Srinivasan, T.N. and Bardhan P.K. (eds.) (1974). Poverty and Income Distribution in India, Statistical Publishing Society, Calcutta.

[17] Suryanarayana, M.H. (1995a). "PDS: Beyond Implicit Subsidy and Urban Bias". *Food Policy*, Vol. 20, No. 4, pp. 259-278.

[18] Suryanarayana, M.H. (1995b), "PDS Reform and Scope for Commodity Based Targeting". *Economic and Political Weekly*, Vol. XXX, No. 13, pp. 687-695.

[19] Suryanarayana, M.H. (1995c), "Some Experiments with Food Stamps", *Economic and Political Weekly,* Vol. XXX, No. 52, pp. A151-A159.

[20] Suryanarayana, M.H. (2009), "Food Security: Beyond the Eleventh Plan Fiction", *International Conference on Health and Development Organized by the School of Development Studies*, Department of Economics, Kannur University. Thalassery and sponsored by the Indian Council of Medical Research, New Delhi, at Thalassery, 22-23 October 2008.

[21] Suryanarayana, M.H. and Silva. D. (2007). "Is Targeting the Poor a Penalty on the Food Insecure? Poverty and Food Insecurity in India", *Journal of Human Development*, Vol. 8, No. 1, pp. 89-106.

[22] Suryanarayana. M.H.(1997). "Food Security in India: Measures, Norms and Issues", *Development and Change*, Vol. 28, No. 4, pp. 771-789.

[23] Suryanarayana, M.H. (1998a). "Methods of Poverty Estimates: A Critical Survey", in Balakrishna, S. and K. Hanumantha Rao (eds.), Data Base on Rural Poverty Indicators, National Institute of Rural Development, Hyderabad.

[24] Suryanarayana, M.H. (2000). "How Real is the Secular Decline in Rural Poverty?" *Economic and Political Weekly*, Vol. XXXV, No. 25, pp. 2129-2139.

[25] Suryanarayana, M.H. (2009a): "Pursuing Inclusion in India: A Story of Specification Errors", *Indian Growth and Development Review*, Vol. 2, No. 2, pp. 155-172.

[26] Suryanarayana. M.H. (2009b). "Policies for the Poor: Verifying the Information Base", Paper for presentation in the Conference on "Quantitative Approaches to Public Policy" in honour of Professor T. Krishna Kumar at the Indian Institute of Management, Bengaluru, 10-12 August 2009.

[27] Tyagi, D.S. (1990) "Increasing Access to Food through Interaction of Price and Technology Policies - The Indian Experience" in Tyagi, D.S. and Vijay Shankar Vyas (eds), *Increasing to Food: The Asian Experience*, pp. 55-98, Sage Publications, New Delhi.

Public Distribution System: Need for Policy Reforms

S.S. Meenakshisundaram

National Institute of Advanced Studies (NIAS)
Indian Institute of Science (IISc) Campus, Bangalore

ABSTRACT

A Public Distribution System (PDS) through fair price shops providing food grains at affordable prices, especially to the poor, has been the key element of the food security system in India for over four decades now. The governance agendas of almost all national governments in India, have been promising to ensure food security for all, and create a hunger free India during their term in office by reforming the PDS, so as to serve the poorest of the poor. With the advent of the new economic policy and the consequent structural adjustment, the role of the PDS became even more crucial. The government cites the system as a safety net for the poor, in the light of the backlash of the changes taking place through globalization, which tend to hit the lower income groups harder. Other opinions however tend towards leaving incomes and quality of life to market forces, in the hope of a positive spillover effects of liberalisation. In this scenario, this article seeks to review the functioning of PDS, in times of both surplus and scarcity, in the context of its role as a safety net for the poor, and suggest suitable policy reforms to make it more effective. The article is in three parts. The first part summarises the salient features of the system, as it exists today. The second contains an analysis of the system, highlighting its strengths and weaknesses, as well as the findings of select research studies on PDS. The final part provides some suggestions and recommendations for policy formulation.

WHAT IS PDS?

PDS in India has a long history. Rationing was first introduced in India in 1939 in Bombay. In 1943, the first Food grain Policy Committee recommended continuation of rationing due to the fall of Burma, which was a major supplier of rice to India, and the great Bengal famine in the preceding year. Immediately after independence, rationing was abolished, only to be reintroduced in 1950, as food shortages led to high prices. The rationing system then introduced due to scarcity of food, later evolved into a full fledged PDS in the mid 1960s, despite near self-sufficiency in food grain production, holding of huge buffer stocks by the government, and rapid expansion of distribution outlets throughout the country. The PDS, over the years, has become an important instrument of government's policy of ensuring availability of food grains to the public at affordable prices, regulating open market prices of essential commodities, and enhancing food security at the household level.

Under the PDS, the Central Government has assumed responsibility for procurement and supply of essential commodities, namely, wheat, rice, sugar, edible oil and kerosene to the states for distribution. These commodities are made available at fixed Central Issue Prices (CIPs), which are determined by the Central Government and generally involve subsidies borne by the Central Government. Some states also distribute additional items of mass consumption through the PDS outlets, called fair price shops (FPSs). The implementation of PDS is the joint responsibility of the central and the state governments. The centre is responsible for procurement, storage and transportation of the commodities up to the central godowns and making them available to the states. The responsibility for distribution to the consumers through the FPSs and administration of the PDS, rests with the state governments.

With a network of around 499,000 FPSs distributing commodities to about 220 million households, India's PDS is perhaps the largest distribution network of its type in the world. The system is designed to help both producers and the consumers of food grains, by linking procurement to support prices, and ensuring their distribution along with other essential commodities at affordable prices throughout the country. This huge network can play a meaningful role, provided the system is able to translate the macro level self-sufficiency, into the micro level availability of food grains for the poor households. Unfortunately, PDS has experienced several implementation problems. It was criticized for the failure to serve below the poverty line (BPL) population, its urban bias, negligible coverage in the states with the highest concentration of rural poor, and lack of transparent and accountable arrangements for delivery. Ostensibly to obviate these short comings, the Government of India streamlined the PDS into a targeted public distribution system (TPDS), so as to improve cost effectiveness in reaching the poor.

The TPDS offers two separate distribution channels, one aimed at BPL households and the other at above poverty line (APL) households. Under the channel for BPL households, the Central Government transfers to the state governments wheat and rice at about half the CIP set for PDS. To start with, monthly ration under the TPDS was kept at 10 kgs per poor household. However, keeping in view the general consensus on increasing the allocation of food grains to BPL families, the Government of India later increased the allocation to 20 kgs per family with effect from 1 April 2000. The allocation of food grains for the BPL families was further increased from 20 kgs to 25 kgs per family per month with effect from July 2001 and to 35 kgs with effect from 1 April, 2002.

Another scheme called the Antyodaya Anna Yojana (AAY) was launched in December, 2000 for 10 million poorest of the poor families. AAY contemplates identification of the poorest of the poor families, from among the BPL families covered under TPDS within the states, and providing them food grains at the highly subsidized rate of Rs. 2 per kg for wheat and Rs. 3 per kg for rice. The scale of issue, which was initially 25 kgs per family per month, was increased to 35 kg per family per month, with effect from 1 April 2002. The AAY scheme was expanded thrice thereafter, by the addition of 5 million BPL households each – first in 2003-04, second in 2004-05 and third in 2005-06, thus increasing its coverage to 25 million households.

Allocation of food grains for the APL category is being made on the basis of availability and stocks in the central pool. Presently, the APL allocations range between 10 and 35 kgs per family per month in different states.

Even though the end retail price is fixed by the States/UTs after taking into account margins for wholesalers/retailers, transportation charges, levies, local taxes, etc., under TPDS and AAY the states were required to issue food grains at a margin of not more than fifty paise per kg over and above the CIP for BPL/AAY families. For APL families, the states can fix the margin keeping in view the actual expenses incurred.

From December 2000, the allocation of food grains for BPL families is being made on the basis of population projections of the Registrar General of Census Operations, as on 1 March 2000 instead of the previous base of projected population of 1995. The identification of the poor is done by the states as per the statewise poverty estimates of the Planning Commission, based on the methodology enunciated by an expert group on "estimation of proportion and number of poor" chaired by the late Prof. Lakdawala. The states also design and implement appropriate targeting mechanisms to reach the poor. The thrust is to include only the really poor and vulnerable sections of society, such as landless agricultural labourers, marginal farmers, rural artisans/craftsmen, urban slum dwellers, urban workers in the informal sectors etc. The state governments, after identifying the poor, issue special cards and deliver food grains to the intended beneficiaries through the FPSs. The Central Government monitors the performance of the states, and the TPDS can even be discontinued if the states do not target and deliver adequately.

Under the second channel, which deals with APL households, the Central Government transfers wheat and rice at CIP, which is usually fixed closer to the market rates. Access through the APL channel is universal. According to the existing guidelines, this channel will be gradually phased out, leaving just the BPL households to be catered by the TPDS/ AAY. Allocation of food grains to the states is based on the average off take of rice and wheat over the previous ten years under PDS. The quantum of food grains in excess of the requirement of BPL families is provided to the states as "transitory allocation," which will be phased out over time.

The Government of India issued a model citizens' charter in November 1997 for adoption by the state governments. It contains essential information, viz., entitlement of BPL families, fair average quality of food grains, information regarding FPS, procedure of issue of ration cards, inspection and checking right to information, vigilance and public participation. In the guidelines issued in June 1999 for the involvement of the Panchayati Raj Institutions (PRIs) in the implementation of the TPDS, it is mentioned that the Gram Panchayat/Gram Sabha should be encouraged to form vigilance committees at the FPS level. The main functions of the vigilance committees are to ensure smooth functioning of PDS, and redressal of related problems.

WHAT DO STUDIES REVEAL?

Has the PDS been effective in meeting the needs of the hungry poor for whose benefit it was designed and implemented, and what has been its impact on household income as well as food security? Several authors and institutions have looked at these questions during the last three decades. The greatest achievement of PDS, to some of these researches, lies in preventing famines in India. PDS has no doubt played a great role by making available rice and wheat at fixed prices to consumers throughout the country. This distribution network also supplied grains for the food for work type programmes taken up on a large scale, to fight droughts and also the normal rural employment programmes. However, the studies also bring out that all is not well with the PDS. The annual food subsidy involved in maintaining the system is huge. It is not cost effective. The ratio between procurement and transportation is high, pointing to wasteful movements sometimes. The storage losses are also high (Nawani, 1994).

A strong criticism of the PDS made out by some authors, is its marginal impact as far as income transfer to poor households is concerned. In a study based on the National Sample Survey's 42nd round in 1990, it was found that "the value of the subsidy is so little even for those households who make all their purchases of cereals from rationshops. For the bottom 20 per cent of the rural population, the subsidy is no more than Rs. 2.08 per capita per 30 days. With the average family size of six, the subsidy per family is almost Rs. 12.50 per month. In other words, it is useful to note here that one person day of additional employment per family per month would provide the same income support as provided by the cereals distributed under PDS" (Parikh, 1994).

The coverage and popularity of the PDS appears to be dependent on the demand and the political, administrative and infrastructural facilities available at the level of the states. Only 33 per cent of the rural households in India have reported use of the PDS on a regular basis. (India Human Development Report, 1999). It is likely that this proportion may fall for short periods of time, such as during the harvesting season. An increase, however, depends on the vibrancy of the programme and regularity of PDS supplies. Available data indicate that the programme is working fairly efficiently in all the four southern states, two western states, and Himachal Pradesh, and at modest levels in Madhya Pradesh. On the other hand, only about five per cent of rural households have reported PDS utilization in Uttar Pradesh (UP), Bihar, Orissa and Punjab. With the exception of Punjab, the other three states have very high levels of under nutrition, both among children and the adult populations. Low PDS utilization in Punjab and Haryana can however be a consequence of lack of demand, since these are agriculturally prosperous states with substantial marketable surpluses. It is significant that the allocation to poorer states like UP Bihar and Assam got more than doubled after the switch-over to TPDS, but the off take by these states was poor and by actual BPL beneficiaries even poorer. The scheme has not made any impact on nutrition levels in these states (Planning Commission, 2000).

Another criticism against the PDS is that the states making the greatest use of the PDS are not necessarily the poorest. Some of the poorer states namely Bihar, Uttar Pradesh and Madhya Pradesh chose to draw a much lower share of PDS subsidies, than what they are entitled to, and also far less than their share of poverty. Targeting within the state is likewise weak. The impact of the PDS as a check on open market food grain prices and as a safety net for the weaker sections of society is also minimal in most of the states, particularly where the per capita distribution is low and social and economic inequalities are more pronounced. With wide variations in the employment situation, consumption levels, percentage of the population below the poverty line etc between the states, it would be difficult to ensure equitable allocation of food grains to different states under the PDS.

A study on the delivery system for PDS in Bihar reported that dealership and even membership of vigilance committees were seen as positions where money can be made. The procedure to appoint them is highly politicized, and mostly clients of MLAs are appointed as dealers. Sub-district infrastructure to handle food grains is poor. (Problems of lack of infrastructure, collusion among officials and shortage of funds with government agencies are not unique to Bihar. Most states suffer such handicaps, except for a few in the West and the South. One study claimed that each fair price dealer has to "maintain" on an average nine government functionaries).

Another weakness pointed out in PDS by several authors, has been its inability to reach the poor effectively. The advent of the TPDS should have remedied the situation. But, the TPDS seems to suffer from the same implementation problems as the PDS. For example, the poor said they were discouraged from using PDS by irregular hours of store operation, lack of information about when rations would be available, insults from shopkeepers and high transport costs, relative to expected savings. The poor in one state complained that by the time they learn of a delivery, most of the grains have already been distributed to the wealthier households living near the shop.

One other drawback that invites abuse and diversion of grains from the poor to the non-poor under the current TPDS, is the expectation that the retail dealer will supply the same variety of grains at half price to the poor (theoretically those with red colour ration cards), and at the regular price to the non-poor. Given past experience with similar arrangements for kerosene and cooking oil (Radhakrishna and Subbarao, 1997), it is unrealistic to expect anything but high levels, of fraud. Although the Central Government plans to enforce strict monitoring, such control is likely to be difficult and administratively costly.

In the wake of several complaints regarding diversion of PDS commodities into the open market, a study was conducted by the Tata Economic Consultancy Services to determine how much of PDS supplies were diverted from the system. At the national level, it was found, there was a diversion of 36 per cent of wheat supplies. 31 per cent of rice and 23 per cent sugar. Statistically at 90 percent confidence level, the actual diversion of wheat would fall in the range of 32-40 per cent, rice in 27-35 per cent and sugar 20-26 per cent. (Planning Commission, 2000) It is significant to note that the diversion is estimated less in the case of sugar, as compared to rice and wheat. The PDS is better organized in towns where sugar is consumed, while its infrastructure is weak in rural areas, especially in the poorer northern, eastern and north eastern states.

A study conducted by ISEC, Bangalore in 2010 on the basis of a large primary survey of 12 states surveying 1,000 households from each state over six consecutive months, still indicates huge identification errors and incidences of diversion of food, especially in the case of households below the poverty line. After consistent field observations over several months, this study has felt that "the delivery of food to the poor was found to be quite regular in the majority of the selected states. For instance, among the Antyodaya households, around 90 per cent (or more) and among the BPL households, around 80 per cent (except Bihar and Assam) received their cereal entitlements quite regularly during the six months of the survey period. The overall delivery efficiency index was above 80 per cent in the five states (in ascending order) of Delhi, Uttarakhand, Rajasthan, Uttar Pradesh and Chhattisgarh, and lowest for Madhya Pradesh (58 per cent) and Bihar (35 per cent). However, deep probing indicated gross idiosyncrasies hidden behind this bright picture. The study observed huge identification errors and some incidences of food diversion, especially in the case of BPL households. The issue of gross failure of identification of the correct beneficiaries found in all the 12 selected states raises the question of whether income cut-off identified through household expenditure, as practised by the Planning Commission, Government of India, is the right methodology for identifying poor families. Other idiosyncrasies observed included excess cards issued/unidentified families; diversion of PDS food; poor quality of food distributed; no system of inspection of entitlements, etc." (Parmod Kumar, 2010).

To summarise, an assessment of the PDS as of now, indicates that while the relevance of PDS as a safety net to the poor has not diminished, the system has confronted several problems such as: identification errors in targeting the poor; complex administration, high administrative costs; poor accountability and beneficiary participation. Though the TPDS and AAY appear to be well targeted, it cannot be said that under this system, food distribution would be regular, adequate and timely. It may also not succeed in meeting the needs of the targeted poor to a significant extent, leading to any notable impact on household incomes, nutrition and food security. This programme which involves huge subsidies may not be cost effective. Finally, there have been no efforts to integrate the ongoing poverty alleviation programmes relating to self employment, wage employment or area development, with the PDS.

WHAT CAN BE DONE?

The PDS no doubt offers great potential for providing extra food to poor households, if only it can successfully reach them. The problem in the identification of the genuine poor looms large. One way to avoid this problem, is to assign a quota to all households (irrespective of whether they arc BPL or APL), as suggested by the National Advisory Council recently. Some experts ridicule this idea and hold a diametrically opposite view. In their opinion, the main weakness in the PDS, viz., not reaching the poor, stems from the universality of its coverage. As of now, every household, irrespective of its income, can have an entitlement card and draw food grains against it under the PDS. This in turn leads to low scales per household, and the first come first served system of delivery. These two combine to allow leakages and diversion on the one hand, and a 'no commitment syndrome' on the part of the poor households on the other. If the PDS could be targeted at the poor, a larger proportion of the household's requirements could be met by enhancing the scale, and it would also be able to generate a commitment on the part of the card holders to the system. Beneficiaries could then be organized and educated. They would then monitor supplies and sales themselves, to ensure that supplies reach the FPSs in proper quantity and quality, and are sold to genuine beneficiaries. The entitled households would also then demand their quota from the FPSs. Targeting of PDS to the really needy therefore appears to be a *sine quo non* for an effective PDS. Though the TPDS may to some extent remedy the situation, the ultimate solution will lie in eliminating the non-poor entirely from the TPDS, and restricting its coverage to the targeted poor only.

Second, for the TPDS to have any nutrition impact, allocation to poor households must be increased. An intake of 10 kgs per household provides an additional 100 calories per person per day, which is inadequate for the poorest households. If the TPDS is to bring caloric levels for the poorest 30 per cent from the current average of about 1500 calories per person per day to even 1900 calories, allocation of an additional 30 kgs of cereals per household is necessary, presuming that the very poor households would maximize their expenditure on food when it is highly subsidized. Provision of additional grains during the months when they are most needed, such as the pre-harvest and rainy seasons, will definitely help in preventing vulnerable children and pregnant women from declining in nutritional status during these periods.

Although rice, wheat, sugar, edible oil, pulses and kerosene are sold through PDS outlets, four of these items namely, rice, wheat, sugar and kerosene account for 86 per cent of the total PDS sales. The share of pulses, the main source of protein for the poor is less than 0.2 per cent. Sugar, rice and kerosene are relatively more important items sold through the PDS in the rural sector, while rice, sugar, kerosene, wheat and edible oils in the urban. Thus there is some basis for the general impression that the composition of PDS commodities is weighted in favour of items supposed to be consumed largely by the relatively richer sections of society (Suryanarayana, 1995). It is therefore necessary to identify the PDS commodities which confer higher income benefits on the poor, through extensive consumer surveys, and to gradually shift those which are used by the non-poor to the open market. To help in the effective transfer of income to the poor, the gap between the issue prices of essential commodities and the market prices can be maintained in such a manner so as to attract the poor to buy PDS commodities.

We need to choose only those foods most consumed by the poor, such as coarse grains and unrefined sugar as transfer instruments for the poor under the PDS. The introduction of coarse grains which are purchased only by the lower income groups, could no doubt help in better targeting, but there are several restricting factors. First, coarse grains are grown by small farmers for their own consumption, and are difficult to collect in sufficient quantities. Second, the production is totally from rainfed lands which may collapse in a drought year. Third, the price of coarse grains is sometimes higher even than that of wheat and rice, and lastly the short shelf life of coarse cereals would not permit their procurement, stocking and distribution through FCI. The only alternative would be to organize grain banks at the village itself, preferably through the PRIs, making use of the local facilities available for stocking and the local FPS for distribution. Such a system can also help in the distribution of food grains at the work spots, wherever rural employment schemes are in operation.

Even if the public distribution of grains is restricted to the targeted poor only, the problem of identifying the genuine poor will remain. This requires strategies which, without ignoring political economy considerations can minimize, if not eliminate the accrual of benefits to the non-poor. A possible solution could be to identify the poor through the Gram sabhas, which have now become an integral part of India's panchayati raj system of local governance. By transferring the task of identification from the bureaucracy to PRIs/ Urban Local Bodies, the selection process will become transparent and access of non-poor to TPDS can be drastically reduced. The plan to issue new cards for households below the poverty line has to be implemented through the PRIs, who can also be given the responsibility to supervise the distribution of cereals through the FPSs within their jurisdiction.

To ensure that the really vulnerable living in the rural areas are covered under TPDS, the criteria for distribution of cards must include: (a) all households participating in the on-going poverty alleviation programmes; (b) single mothers with children or widows without support; (c) all non-income tax paying households; (d) small and marginal farmers; and (e) all landless agricultural labourers and petty artisans who can be identified in open Gram Sabha meetings. The running of the grain banks wherever established through local purchase of coarse grains, can also be entrusted to the village panchayats. This will ensure market friendly procurement, local storage and timely utilization. Discussions on procurement, stocking and distribution policies at the village panchayat/Gram Sabha levels will greatly enhance participation of the beneficiaries in food security measures, besides ensuring transparency.

Even after taking all necessary steps to exclude the non-poor under TPDS, there can still be the possibility of its being usurped in time by those who do not require subsidized food. To prevent this, a few more safety mechanisms have to be designed. For instance, the contracts for FPSs can be given to community groups, particularly women self-help groups, and cooperatives as against individuals. These shops will have to be located in areas where the poor and the vulnerable live. Participation by the beneficiary groups must be insisted upon, both in the location of shops and also in their actual running. The performance of the FPS must also be put down as a subject for discussion during the meetings of the gram sabha.

As the implementation of the PDS is carried out though FPSs, the economic viability of these shops is relevant to the efficient functioning of the system, as well as curbing malpractices such as diversion of commodities to the open market. Particularly in rural areas, the poor return on investments made by FPS owners does not make the business, attractive. It may perhaps be necessary to encourage them to have their own business in addition to the distribution of commodities under PDS. Further, if the distribution of PDS is organized on a weekly basis as in Kerala, the invested capital would be continuously utilized, and only smaller amounts of cash would be required for working capital at any time. From the purchasers point of view also, a weekly system of allotment would be much more beneficial, as many of the poor families cannot afford to purchase their whole entitlement in the few days when stocks are available.

Finally, greater emphasis on consumer awareness, rather than official vigilance committees may be more effective in streamlining the PDS. People can exercise effective checks and controls on the functioning of the PDS, as is evident from the example of Kerala. The existence of a large number of grassroot level organizations will also provide adequate foray for consumer complaints and their timely redressal.

Linking the TPDS with the Mahatma Gandhi National Rural Employment Guarantee Scheme (MGNREGS) can be a useful option, because in such programmes, the poor can derive a double benefit. First, the error of inclusion of non-poor is minimised, since non-poor generally do not come for employment under these programmes. Second, besides transferring purchasing power in the hands of the poor through employment generation, additional income transfers can also take place through PDS supplies to the participants.

While taking up employment programmes, it may be desirable to allot a proportion of food grains exclusively for women. This will ensure that more women participate in these programmes, and that they are not excluded, because of physical or traditional gender segregation of the work activities. All workers, rather than only one member of the family, must be made eligible for rations, when they work in such projects. This will ensure that women who work alongside their male family members get equal opportunities to receive food grains directly. This will also result in the children of the family getting the required food.

The state governments or the PRIs can also distribute food stamps/vouchers to the workers employed under these programmes, which can be utilized to purchase food grains from the local FPSs. Since the responsibility to execute the employment generation programmes is now vested with the PRIS, it would not be difficult for the PRIs to link these programmes with the local FPS for distribution of a portion of the wages in the form of grains. To check deviations from the intended purpose by the PRIs/FPSs and also at the work spots, it would be useful if NGOs with a proven record of helping the poor are involved in supervising the entire procedure.

In a country where there is mass poverty, where food consumption is low, and where expenditure on food accounts for the bulk of the total family expenditure is high we need to expand and strengthen, and not undermine and disband the PDS. Its utility as a safety net for the poor is beyond doubt. Unfortunately, the implementation of PDS has been rather tardy. There are large differences in the coverage and functioning of PDS across the states. This is not surprising, given the differences in the class character and politics of different state governments. While strong political support is essential to establish and maintain the PDS, good governance seems to hold the key to make it an effective safety net for the poor.

REFERENCES

[1] Nawani N.P. (1994). Indian Experience on Households Food and Security. Paper presented for regional expert consultation FAO-UN, Bangkok.

[2] Parikh. K., (1994). "Who Gets How Much from PDS: How Effectively Does it Reach the Poor?" Sarvekshana, January-March.

[3] Suryanarayana, M.H., (1995). 'Growth, Poverty and Levels of Living: Hypotheses, Methods and Policy', *Journal of Indian School of Political Economy*, 7, 2, April-June.

[4] Radhakrishna, Rokkam, and Subbarao, K., (1997), 'India's Public Distribution System: A National and International Perspective' Discussion paper No. 380, Washington, D.C., World Bank.

[5] *Mid Term Appraisal of Ninth Five Year Plan, 2000*, Planning Commission, Government of India, New Delhi, October.

[6] *Report of the Tenth Plan Working Group on Public Distribution System and Food Security, 2001*, Ministry of Consumer Affairs, Government of India, New Delhi.

[7] *Performance Evaluation of TPDS, (2005), Programme Evaluation Organisation*, Planning Commission, Government of India, New Delhi.

[8] *Annual Report 2009-10*, Ministry of Consumer Affairs, Food and Public Distribution, Government of India, New Delhi.

[9] Parmod Kumar, (2010), "Functioning of the Public Distribution System in India: An empirical evaluation", *Outlook on Agriculture*, Vol. 39, No. 3.

Market-led Extension Models for Farmers' Empowerment

K.R. Viswambharan, P.J. George[1] and P. Ahamed[2]

Kerala Agricultural University, Kerala
[1]Sam Higginbottom Institute of Agriculture, Technology and Sciences, Allahabad
[2]Centre for E-Learning, Kerala Agricultural University, Kerala

ABSTRACT

An effective and efficient system of agricultural marketing is the need of the hour to protect farmers from middlemen. Presence of an organized production and marketing set up is essential for the farmers' empowerment. The study is mainly targeted to suggest strategic models for initiating farmer-led self help groups and marketing federations in Kerala and other Indian states, based on the constraints and SWOC analyses of the present system. The study contributes strategic tips for better streamlining of the SHG attempts.

The ex post facto research design used a blend of tools like survey and participatory appraisals. The study especially covered Farmers' Organizations (FOs); SHGs; Farmers' Interest Groups (FIGs); Commodity Interest Groups (CIGs) and Market-led Extension. The study has established that the production and market intervention of Vegetable and Fruit Promotion Council Keralam (VFPCK) through its SHGs, and their farmers' market federations have benefited farmers through increased social interaction, increased bargaining power, better knowledge, skill and attitude, better group market culture, better prices and sustainable profits. The SWOC analysis revealed a set of high-ranked opportunities like strengthening linkages with R&D, crop diversification, market diversification, intensive intercropping, building storage facilities, produce diversification, value addition and processing, export, training in frontier areas, small farm mechanization, labour pool and labour banks, and better scientific seed production programmes.

The study has contributed two inter related alternative marketing models namely, the societal marketing model, and the SHGs-linked farmers' market model. The former model highlights the overall empowerment of the farmer producers, and the societal advantages to the consumers. The latter market model highlights the importance of crop producing SHGs getting federated as farmers' markets, with an additional focus on crop diversification, diversification of marketable produce, storage, and post harvest processing establishment of the retail outlet chain for graded and standardized farm fresh products, targeting premium segments, and exporting. Both the models suggest that the fruits and vegetable-producing tracts should draw action plans for facilitating the formation of SHGs and their federated markets for direct marketing of the produce, arranging suitable finance from different sources, and giving all types of technical assistance to such groups for sustainable growth.

Keywords: Market-led Extension, Marketing Models, Societal Marketing Model, SHGs-Linked Farmers' Market Model, Farmers' Empowerment.

INTRODUCTION

India is the world's twelfth largest economy in USD exchange rate terms. India is the second fastest growing economy in the world. India's GDP touched US$1.25 trillion in 2007. This has put the country in the elite group of 12 countries with trillion dollar economies. The tremendous growth rate has coincided with better macroeconomic stability. India has made remarkable progress in information technology, high-end services and knowledge process services. Still, the momentous role that agriculture continues to play in the nation's economic growth is unquestionable. Whatever the economic structure has been in the past or is today, undoubtedly India's economy will continue to be based on agriculture in the foreseeable years. A vibrant agriculture in India is central to the well being of the largest section of the population living in rural villages, as well as for the welfare of the urban population. Even though the contribution of agriculture to India's Gross Domestic Product (GDP) has been declining for the last fifteen years, this primary sector persists as the single largest contributor to the GDP, to the tune of 16.9 per cent.

India being a 'land of peasants', it is quite paradoxical that today the service sector is contributing more than half of the Indian GDP. It is the service sector that takes India one step closer to the developed economies of the world. Earlier it was agriculture, which mainly contributed to the GDP of India.

India's progress in the agricultural sector has been enormous since the dawn of independence over 63 years ago. Productivity has increased over three folds compared to 1950. The country has achieved self-sufficiency in food grains production and is even able to export. The diversity of topography, physical endowment, climatic factors and human resources preclude a fair quantification of the role of agriculture in the socio-economic development of the country as a whole. Despite these, the retarded growth of the agriculture sector has cast a shadow over the overall development of the country.

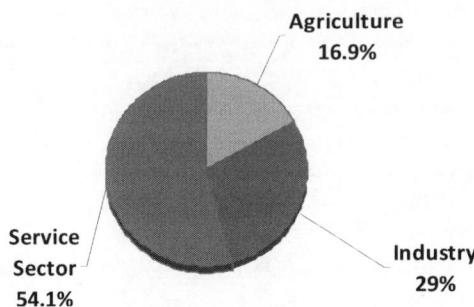

Fig. 1. Contribution of Various Sectors to the GDP of India (2008-09)

Unorganized sectors like vegetables, fruit crops, herbs, medicinal plants, and such others, face inadequate organized support or institutional systems for technology, credit and trade. Small farms, homestead farms and subsistence/poor farmers mostly are in this unorganized sector. They are vulnerable to middlemen in the trade, and are too feeble by themselves to influence the market. Besides better support for market returns, they also need better support for knowledge, skill, attitude and technology inputs. Thus, there is great scope at the levels of production, technology use, post harvest, and marketing improvisations.

Agricultural marketing in India is basically in the clutches of middlemen, whose practices are often exploitative and the cultivators are always the worst hit. The cultivation of fruits and vegetables is at the mercy of the middlemen more than other crops, because of the highly perishable nature of the produce, coupled with the imperfect market structure ruled by unscrupulous intermediaries. An effective and efficient system of agricultural marketing is the need of the hour to protect farmers from the middlemen. All these call for an organized marketing setup, focusing on the 'cultivator's advantage'. Here comes the practicality of a farmer- led marketing system.

France, Norway and Taiwan provide examples of the prominent role farmers' organizations can play in funding and organizing agricultural extension (Haug, 1991; Ameur, 1994; Umali and Schwartz, 1994; Nagel, 1997). Consultants from a number of fields, together with farm-supply industries, general farm and commodity organisations, and the farm press, routinely delivered information to farmers that were previously delivered primarily by governmental extension (Bloome, 1992). NGOs have made considerable-impact on the development of the rural poor, as well as dissemination of technologies (Chambers and Toulmin, 1992).

On the role of farmers' organizations, Chris and Nicola (1997) reported that a strong structure of farmers' organizations could offer an opportunity for greater efficiency, effectiveness and equity of provision and access. They could also be a vehicle through which farmers could pay a contribution for services, become actively involved in the planning and management of extension, and act as a voice for their members, in getting services which meet their needs.

MARKETING: CONCEPT AND METHODS

Market is an operationalized atomistic realm of impersonal economic exchange of goods and services by voluntary transactions, mediated by a large number of autonomous fully informed entities, with the motive of free entry and exit. Philip Kotler, the father of modern marketing, defined marketing, as a societal process by which individuals and groups obtain what they need and want through creating, offering, and freely exchanging products and services of value with others. He further defined marketing management as the analysis of planning, implementation and control of programs designed to create, build and maintain beneficial exchange with target buyers, for the purpose of achieving organizational objectives. Marketing management philosophies include production, products, selling, marketing and societal marketing (Kotler and Armstrong, 1997).

CONCEPTS OF MARKETING MANAGEMENT

1. *Production concept:* This concept holds that the consumer will favour products that are available and highly affordable. Therefore, management should focus on improving production and distribution efficiency. The production concept is a useful philosophy in situations when demand for a product exceeds supply, and when the product's cost is too high and improved productivity is needed to bring it down.

2. *Product concept:* This concept holds that consumers will favour products that offer the most quality, performance and innovative features, and that the organization should therefore devote its energy to making continuous improvements. It is a detailed version of the new product idea stated in meaningful consumer terms.

3. *Selling concept:* This concept holds that consumers will not buy enough of the organizations products unless the organization undertakes large scale selling and promotion efforts. The product is typically practiced with unsought goods. The aim is to sell what they make, rather than make what the market wants.

4. *Marketing concept:* This concept holds that achieving organizational goals depends on determining the needs and wants of the target market and delivering the desired good.

5. *Societal marketing concept*: This concept holds that the organization should determine the needs, wants and interests of the target markets. It should then deliver superior value to customers in a way that maintains or improves the consumer's and the society's well-being. This concept calls upon marketers to balance three considerations in setting their marketing policies: company profits, consumer wants and society's interests.

AGRICULTURAL MARKETING SYSTEM AND CONSTRAINTS

Agricultural marketing includes the movement of agricultural produce from farms where it is produced to the consumers or manufactures. This covers physical handling and transport, initial processing and packing to simplify handling and reduce wastage, grading and quality control to simplify sales transactions and meet different consumers' requirements, and holding over time to match concentrated harvest seasons, with the continuing demands of consumers throughout the year. For the farmer, the strategic function of the marketing system is to offer him convenient outlets for his produce at a remunerative price. To the consumers and the manufactures of agricultural raw materials, assurance of a steady supply at a reasonable price is the vital service. Prices are determined through the free market process by negotiations for rural purchase, wholesale and retail stages, and represents a balance between the consumers' ability to pay and the farmers need for incentives to produce (Skoppek, 2006). An effective marketing system will be geared towards expanding the range and types of consumer service, and thus offer procurement outlets.

An efficient marketing system is vital for providing an incentive to the farmers to produce more, convey the changing production needs of the economy to producers to enable production planning, and foster true competition among the traders and eliminate the exploitation of farmers, particularly the small and marginal ones, who predominate the agrarian sector in our country.

In a vibrant society, the marketing system has to be dynamic, and this is possible only by undertaking continuous search for making it most efficient and effective, in order to maximize the welfare of the consumers as well as producers of agricultural products, (Bhatia, 1995). suggested various measures for improving the agricultural marketing system which includes suitable pricing policies, active participation of public procurement agencies, strengthening of cooperatives, scientific grading, credit linked storage, storage facilities at reasonable cost, improved market intelligence and systematic and continuous estimation of demand for various agricultural products (Murthy and Reddy,1996). Timely and accurate market information is the base for an efficient marketing system. Taking advantage of the technological and scientific advancements, the state agriculture marketing boards and departments shall take up collection and dissemination of market information on prices, demand, and supply movements (Bhat, 2001) . One possible way of improving agricultural marketing is to bring a meaningful model, beneficial for both farmers and industrialists, by inviting farmer's participation in equity in agricultural production/processing ventures. This will transform the corporate sector into a cooperative sector. Thus, the farmers could retain their land and do farming in their own land, and the cooperative provides them some key inputs and sound marketing support (Barbora, 2001).

Kurien (2007), based on a socio-economic study on the management of the marketing system for perishable agricultural commodities in Kerala, summarized that participatory decision making, supplemented by transparent marketing management, improved the efficiency and transparency of farmer led markets. He stressed the imperative role the farmers' group markets can play in making the small and medium farmers thrive on their own, by shielding them from the exploitation of intermediaries and monopolization of multinational companies in the agricultural sector in this era of globalization.

While studying the functioning of group marketing of fruits and vegetables in Kerala, he reported that farmers are assured of a regular market, fair price, better weights and measures, standardized grading materials, need based training and timely marketing information by the VFPCK. The 'Group Marketing' system followed by the VFPCK is a paradigm shift in marketing, as the traders are made to come to the farmers market, instead of the farmers going after the traders. In fact, the VFPCK has been able to liberate the farmers from the unfair trade practices of the unscrupulous middlemen, and to a great extent restore the self esteem of the cultivators of the soil. Farmers as well as traders are satisfied with the functioning of the SKS. Farmers are saved the trouble of taking their produce to distant markets, incurring a number of marketing costs and assuming several risks. Traders are assured of quality produce at fair prices, in large quantities. The SKS markets have enabled a considerable number of poor landless cultivators to take up fruits and vegetables commercially by extending membership to them. Through an integrated approach to farmers, the VFPCK has been able to empower the farmers socially and economically (Mohan (2007).

The present article forms a part of the study done to evaluate the performance of the SHG systems, and how they impinge on the rural agricultural economy and livelihoods of the farmers of Kerala; and how best some of these models could be extrapolated to the other Indian states, with suitable temporal and spatial modifications.

METHODOLOGY

Ex post facto research design was used for the study. The study was done in four phases in nine selected districts of Kerala. The study was conducted in two stages: Field survey in 2008-09 and participatory assessment in 2009-10. A blend of judgment/criteria-based multistage stratified random sampling method was followed. The study used 189 SHGs drawn from nine districts for Stage I. Each SHG was represented by one Key Informant (KI) from among the master farmers. Thus, the final sample of the study comprised 189 units (i.e. 189 master farmers representing 189 SHGs).

For the third phase of the study, Participatory Learning and Action (PLA) method was used for 'the key informant workshop' to analyze the performance of the farmers' markets (SKSs). PLA tools like semi structured interviewing, brain storming, preference scoring and ranking and Venn diagramming were used.

RESULTS AND SUGGESTIONS

Need for Group Based Approach to Agricultural Production and Marketing

When people work in groups and try to solve their problems jointly,they achieve success. For most individual, social, economic and agricultural activities, rural society has evolved several group methods and approaches to mutually solve their problems and render help and support to each other. Such group activities exist in every rural society. There is a need to identify such group activities, and understand their mutual interests, as well as group dynamics for agricultural and rural development. The group approach provides strength in solving agricultural problems and making farm business more income and employment oriented. Self Help Group (SHG) approaches already exist, which emphasize on participation at the grassroot level through local group formation. Farmer groups collectively analyze the local markets, and emerge as pressure groups to effectively negotiate with mainstream support agencies to access resources. Farmers' groups are also encouraged to put pressure on the government officials to provide fertilizers, high yielding variety of seeds, irrigation, credit, minimum support price for food grains, market facilities, crop insurance, and scientific agricultural expertise from resource agencies.

Strategic Models for Initiating Farmer-led Self Help Groups and Farmers' Markets

One of the strategic objectives of the present investigation entitled "Role of self help groups in the development and management of sustainable agricultural programmes in Kerala state" was to suggest suitable and strategic models for initiating farmer-led self help groups, and farmers' marketing federations in Kerala and other Indian states.

Based on an analysis of the history and formation of self help groups, surveys and participatory assessment of the functioning of farmers' market federations of the VFPCK, and the results of the SWOC analysis contributed the conceptual, theoretical and practical contents for building the strategic models. Accordingly, two models were designed, as described now.

Societal Marketing Concept Model for Sustainable Farmers' Market

The model presented in Fig. 2 is based on the overall perspective that emerged from the present study. It has partially borrowed a few ideas of the contrasts in the selling concept and marketing concept highlighted by Kotler and Armstrong (1997). The 'marketing concept' holds that achieving organizational goals, depends on determining the needs and wants of the target market and delivering the desired produce to the customer.

The selling concept takes an inside out perspective. It starts with the production centre, focuses on the company's existing products, and calls for heavy selling and promotion to obtain profitable sales. It focuses heavily on customer conquest. In contrast, the marketing concept takes an outside in perspective. It starts with a well defined market, focuses on customer needs, coordinates all the marketing activities affecting customers, and makes profits by creating long term customers, relationships based on customer value and satisfaction.

The societal marketing model proposed in the present study for initiating farmers' SHGs and their market federations is one more step ahead. This model aims at the farmers' and organization's empowerment, making use of the societal marketing concept. The model holds that the farmers' market federation should facilitate members to produce to cope with the demands of the traders, the market, the consumers and the temporal and local trends and demands for fruits and vegetables. It should then deliver superior value to customers in a way that maintains or improves the consumer's and society's well-being. This model calls upon the SKSs to balance three considerations in setting their marketing policies: farmers' profits, consumers' wants and society's interests.

The model also highlights the importance of a cognitive domain, i.e. agriculture experimentation and learning, while producing and marketing. Here, agriculture learning is operationalised as the farmers' SHGs, and farmers' markets accessing new technologies (may be new crops or varieties, or new knowledge or new equipment, or new marketing techniques) for their own evaluation. The assumption is that technologies are available with the research and extension system, of interest and value to farmers – if only they knew of them and could access them. And that, with support, farmers' groups and farmers' market federations can access and evaluate these new technologies and make decisions to adopt, adapt or reject. That is the kind of 'learning' envisaged by the proposed model.

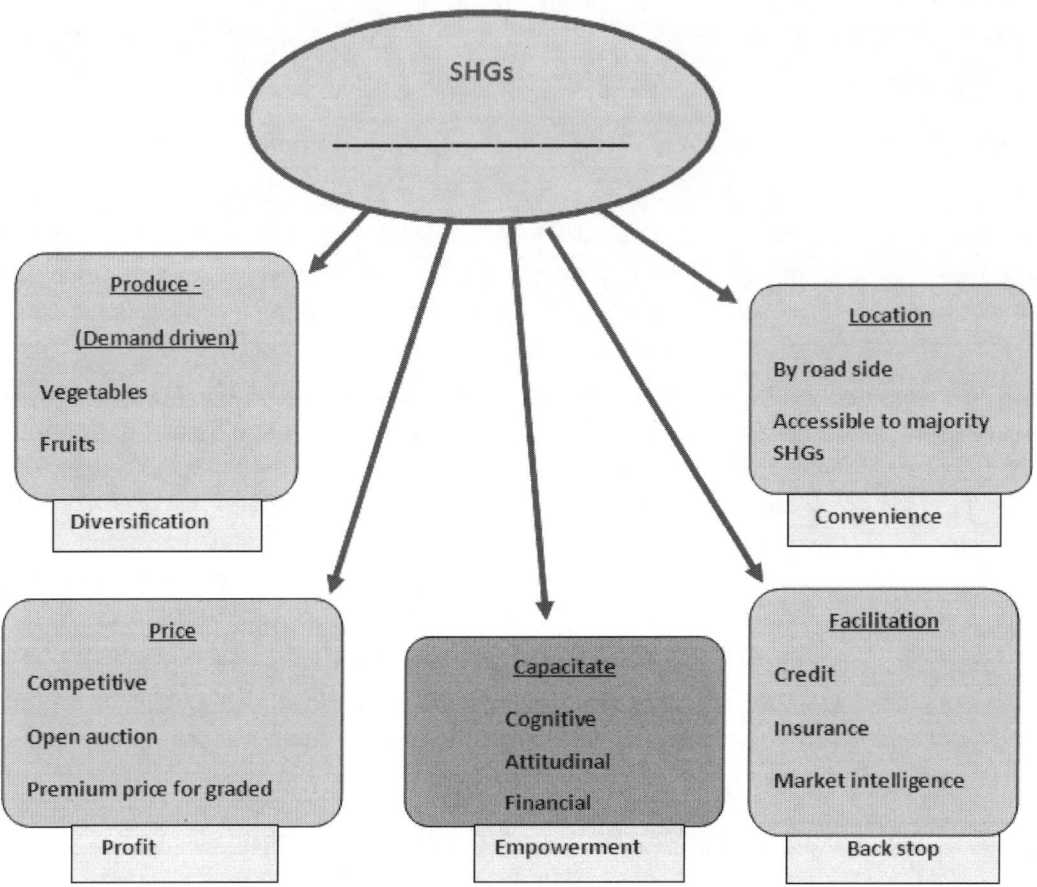

Fig. 2. Societal Marketing Concept Model for Sustainable Farmers' Market

The farmer's market should be ideally located, should ensure transparency in pricing, and should provide a congenial atmosphere for trading and participation. The price is to be fixed based on market price by auction or bargain. Price should be in accordance with grades and quality. Instead of the orthodox 'selling' concept, a societal marketing concept is recommended. There should be a balance of farmers' profits, consumers' wants, farmers' and organization's capacity building and empowerment, and society's interests. Derivation of profit should be by integrated marketing, produce diversification, value addition and customer satisfaction. A facilitating type of back stopping by the umbrella organization is proposed.

SHGs-Linked Farmers' Market Model

As illustrated in Fig. 3, groups of small and marginal vegetable farmers operating in a continuous area are brought together under an umbrella agency like the VFPCK/a government scheme/*Kudumbashree*/voluntary agency/NABARD/farmers' consortium./a bank/or an NGO. The farmers are oriented as an SHG in groups of 10-20, or a convenient size. Group leaders are selected on a democratic basis, without considering any political, religious, or any other kind of group disparity. The SHGs will convene regular meetings, which shall act as a forum for discussions and actions for mutual benefit. Plans and schedules for inputs procurement, cultural operations, irrigation facilities, and post harvest operations will be discussed and action plans prepared. Responsibilities are delegated in the form of Lead Farmer (Production), Lead Farmer (Credit), Lead Farmer (Marketing), and the like, to coordinate and facilitate group actions in the respective areas. Other lead farmers may be appointed such as Lead Farmer (Logistics), Lead Farmer (Storage) as per the requirements of the group. These SHGs will be federated to a farmers' market (like the *Swashraya Karshaka Samithi* of VFPCK). The farmers' market will have a professional agricultural field expert, from the umbrella organization for transfer of technology, and to advise the SHGs under the federation and to help the farmers' markets on production, management and marketing. The farmers' market federation will have a democratically elected body as non-official office bearers for a term of 2-3 years. The team will be changed so as to give other farmers a chance to use their leadership ability.

The SHGs will draw up market demand-oriented production plans, and allocate mutually acceptable production plans for individual farmers. The group facilitated by the lead farmer, will adopt the latest production technologies, and will cultivate such crops that have a definite market segment demand. Input procurement and production issues will be handled on a collective basis. Group members will participate in research, extension and training programmes. Master farmers will train fellow farmers. A 'farmer to farmer extension' approach will be followed. Besides profits, the motto will be similar to that of the VFPCK: "Self help, participation, and prosperity" with an added dimension – overall empowerment of the farmers.'

The harvested produce on the basis of market demand is pooled in a common place, preferably at the "Farmers' Market" (e.g. *Swashraya Karshaka Samithi* of VFPCK), wherein the farmers collectively bargain with the traders. There is no foul play by middleman. Farmers get reasonable market prices. A retail wing of the farmers' market to cater to nearby cities serving graded fruits and vegetables will help them in getting premium prices. Effective forward and backward linkages with transport operators, cold storage operators and value addition centres are possible, to avert surplus production, so as to prevent any market glut, and resultant price reductions. A regulated market flow through scientific storage ensures regular income spread over longer periods.

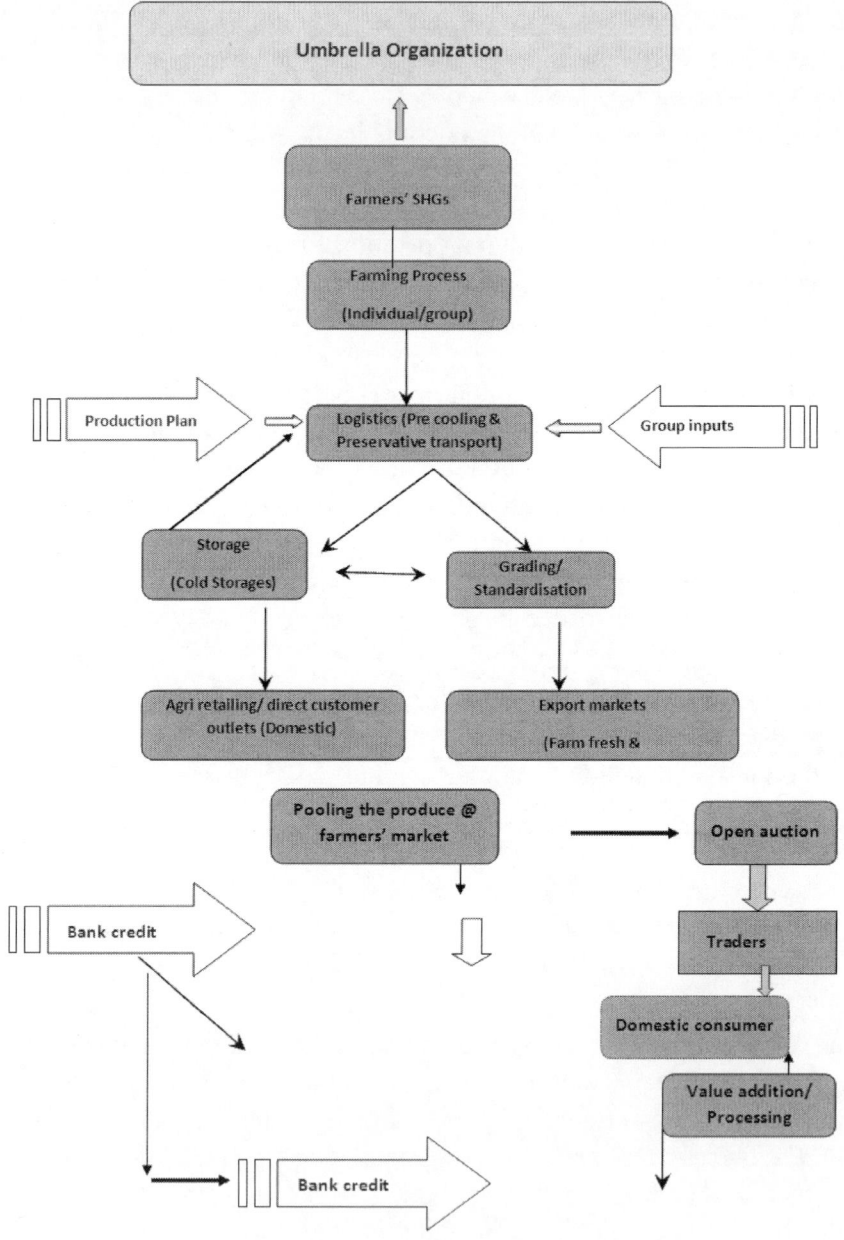

Fig. 3. SHGs-linked Farmers' Market Model

Future prospects of such farmers' market federation lies in diversification. After successful establishment, the farmers' market can open refrigeration/pre cooling centres of their own to minimize postproduction losses. The next step will be the establishment of a retail outlet chain for graded and standardised farm fresh products, targeting super/hyper markets, or other premium segments. The federation can finally enter into value addition, processing and branding, to enter into the export market to create a self-sustainable system.

Bankers are ready to help such farmers' groups. It starts with production and investment credit for member farmers. Through the forward and backward linkages of the groups, banks are ready to finance transport operators, handlers, cold storages, retailing chains and value addition centres.

Such a farmers' market federation is a future model for sustainable agricultural development in Kerala and India. Even though already proved by the VFPCK for vegetables and fruits, the same can be done for any crop with suitable modifications. The same can be an ideal even for the food grain farmers who are always at the receiving end. The contents of the societal marketing concept model shown in Fig. 3 of this article has to be super imposed with the SHGs-linked farmers' market model.

Thus, by using a logical blend of the two models, the sidelined group of small and marginal farmers, using their strength of unity, can be helped to stay competitive in changing market environment. It is a great process of viable business propositions from the so-called non-viable groups.

SUMMARY AND CONCLUSION

Based on the results that emerged from the present study, two marketing models were conceived, namely, the societal marketing model, and the SHGs-linked farmers' market model.

The societal model aims at farmers' and organization's empowerment, making use of the societal marketing concept. The model holds that the farmers' market federation should facilitate members to produce crops to cope with the demands of traders, the market, the consumers and the temporal and local trends, and demands for fruits and vegetables. The model also highlights the importance of a cognitive domain, i.e. agriculture experimentation and learning. The SHGs-linked farmers' market model highlights the importance of crop producing SHGs getting federated as a "Farmers" Market like that of the VFPCK approach. But the present model provides an additional focus for crop diversification, diversification of marketable produce, storage, and post harvest processing establishment of retail outlet chains for graded and standardized farm fresh products, targeting premium segments, and for exporting.

Based on the organizational and management aspects, and results emerging from the study, the following areas related to group dynamism, human relationships, leadership, and efficient marketing management may be taken care of by such SHGs and farmers' markets:

1. Identifying roles and responsibilities of executives and members of the groups.

2. Streamlining the constitutional and functional norms of such groups and farmers' markets.

3. Equipping members with techniques of organizing and functioning of the SHGs and markets.

4. Participatory decision making, accounting and financial management in a transparent manner

5. Developing leadership with changing roles and responsibilities on a gender basis.

6. Developing interpersonal relationships and mutual trust.

7. Mobilizing internal as well as external resources.

8. Developing a comprehensive marketing strategy using a blend of the societal marketing model and the SHGs-linked marketing model, as proposed in the present study.

9. Promotion / enforcement of open auctions in the markets.

10. Direct participation of farmers should be increased.

11. Market infrastructure should be improved through facilities like storages/godowns, cold storages, and processing facilities.

12. Improvement of the road network, and cold chain facilities.

13. Greater transparency of operations through supervision and systems.

14. Market integration and efficiency can also be improved by making up-to-date market information available to all participants through various means, including a good market information system, internet and good telecommunication facilities in the market.

ACKNOWLEDGEMENTS

The authors sincerely wish to record the motivation, help and support provided for this investigation by Rev. Prof. (Dr.) Rajendra B. Lal, the Hon'ble Vice-Chancellor and the Faculty of the Sam Higginbottom Institute of Agricultural Technology and Sciences (SHIATS), Allahabad; the Chief Executive Officer of the Vegetables and Fruits Promotion Council Keralam (VFPCK) and the office bearers, master farmers and other member farmers of the SHGs and farmers' markets of the VPCK.

REFERENCES

[1] Ameur, C. (1994). *Agricultural Extension: A Step beyond the Next Step.* World Bank Technical Paper No.247, The World Bank, Washington DC, 47. p.

[2] Barbora, S. (2001) Agricultural marketing needs dynamism (ed. Vedini, K.H.). Agric. Marketing. National Institute of Agricultural Extension Management, Hyderabad. pp. 63-71.

[3] Berdegue, J.A. 1990. *NGOs and farmers' organizations in research and extension in Chile.* Agricultural Administration, Research and Extension Network Paper No. 19. Overseas Development Institute, London, p. 17

[4] Bhat, M.K.V. 2001. Amendments to agricultural produce markets acts (ed. Vedini, K.H.). *Agriculture Marketing. Interventions and Innovations.* National Institute of Agricultural Extension Management, Hyderabad. pp. 38-44.

[5] Bhatia, G.R. (1995). Rapid assessment of agricultural marketing system in India. *Agric. Marketing.* 37(4): 16-26.

[6] Bloome, P.D. (1992). *Seeking a Mature Relationship with Agriculture* [On-line].Available:http.//:www.joe.org/joe/ 1992spring/tpi.html. [15 January, 2010].

[7] Chambers, R. and Toulmin, C. (1992). Farmers first: Achieving sustainable dry land development in Africa. *Rural Households in Emerging Societies: Technology and Change in Sub-Saharan Africa* (eds. Maryaret, A.S. and Hunt, D.). Oxford Berg Publishers, New York, pp. 158-160.

[8] Haug, R. 1991 . Public-private co-operation: Farmer-led research/ extension circles in Norway. *Agricultural Extension: Worldwide Institutional Innovation and Forces for Change* (eds. Rivera, W.M. and Gustafson, D.J.). Elsevier, Amsterdam, pp. 116-129.

[9] Kotler, P. and Armstrong, G. (1997). *Principles of Marketing.* Prentice Hall Inc. USA. pp. 3-22.

[10] Kurian, B.K. 2008 . Management of marketing system for oerishable agriculture commodities in Kerala: problems and prospects. Ph.D. Thesis, Mahathma Gandhi University, Kottaya, Kerala. p. 205.

[11] Mohan, B. 2007 . Group marketing system for fruits and vegetables in Kerala. MSc (C&B) thesis, Kerala Agricultural University, Thrissur, p. 135.

[12] Murthy, N. and Reddy, K.R. (1996). Some observations of' about the changing environment of agricultural marketing, in India: *Indian Journal of Marketing.* 25(4): 20-24.

[13] Nagel, U.J. (1997). Alternative approaches to organizing extension. *Improving Agricultural Extension: A Reference Manual* (eds. Swanson, B.C., Bentz, R.P. and Sofranko, L.A.J.). Food and Agricultural Organization, Rome, pp. 11-2.9

[14] Roling, N. (1988). *Extension Science: Information Systems in Agricultural Development.* Cambridge University Press, Cambridge.

[15] Swanson, R E., Bentz, R.P. and Sofranko, A.J. 1990 . *Improving Agricultural Ext iension: A Reference Manual.* Food and Agricultural Organization. p. 220.

Sub-National Reforms in Punjab: Public Policy vs. Populism

Upinder Sawhney and Amrita Shergill

Department of Economics, Panjab University, Chandigarh

ABSTRACT

The economic reforms implemented in the Indian economy have initiated a lot of academic, political and social debate within and outside India, over the last two decades. The purpose of economic reforms was to bring about efficiency, transparency and effectiveness of governments at all levels – union, state and local. However, the wave of economic reforms brought about significant changes at the national level, but the other two layers of government , i.e., state and local, have not shown much dynamism in the reform process.

Some states of the Indian Union have witnessed economic progress by adopting reforms at the state level, but there are certain laggard states, including the leading one like Punjab, which have not shown any considerable effectiveness of the reform process. The state did not rise to bring about any major changes for many years and pursued populist policies, which led to a major fiscal crisis and economic deceleration in the state. The Government of Punjab (GOP) had to finally wake up to the need for certain reforms including fiscal, institutional as well as the reforms in the state level public enterprises (SLPEs). The present article seeks to evaluate the extent of reforms in the state in the last two decades, and will examine its success or otherwise, as well as the further need for economic and governance reforms in Punjab.

Keywords: Reforms, Sub-National, Governance.

INTRODUCTION

The Indian economy has undergone a paradigm shift in its economic policies since the mid-1980s. Successive reforms and reduction of state intervention and control over economic activity have progressively moved the economy towards a market-based system, and have brought about deregulation, decontrol and openness in the economy. The rate of growth of the economy which was 2-3 per cent since Independence up to the end of the 1970s, has gone over 7 per cent in the last decade and a half. Liberalization of economic policy has had an impact on most aspects of the economic policy, including industrial and trade policies, foreign investment policy, fiscal policy, financial market reforms and public sector restructuring. The target of the government to attain 10 percent growth of the Gross Domestic Product (GDP) is achievable, if reforms continue.

In a federal set-up, the relevance of policy reforms at the national level is undermined if its sub-national constituents do not make efforts towards economic betterment through institutional and policy reforms, in tune with the national policies. Therefore, the Indian states must create an enabling environment for the implementation and success of the macro economic reforms and the structural adjustment programme adopted by the Government of India (GoI) in 1991. State level fiscal consolidation and responsibility, creation of better infrastructure and effective governance are the prerequisites for the success of sub-national reforms. However, sub national reforms in India have been largely neglected, and not much discussed in academic or political forums. It has been established widely that state-level reforms in India have been uneven throughout the country, and the success or failure of the same has been largely determined by the quality of governance at the level of each state of the Indian union.

Research into state-level reforms is still not enough, compared to work on the progress and review of national economic reforms. There have been some studies by Callebaut, (1997), Ahluwalia (2000), Howes, Lahiri and Stern (2004), The World Bank Report (2005), Sawhney (2005), Nambiar (2007, 2010), etc. Most of the work at the sub-national level, relates to fiscal reforms and a lot of work on this aspect has been done by the scholars at The National Institute of Public Finance and Policy, New Delhi. No doubt, fiscal responsibility of the state governments in India needs to be scrutinized closely, but other areas like the public sector (notably power sector) reforms, infrastructure development commensurate with national development policies and issues relating to the efficiency, effectiveness and transparency of government activities have been largely ignored. The present article seeks to examine the pace and pattern of sub-national reforms in Punjab, one of the most developed states in India. It is important to study this, in view of the deteriorating economic condition of the state over the last few years. The study assumes significance in view of the fact, that the institutional framework to facilitate the reforms has been updated and restructured from time to time by the Government of Punjab (GOP), but the economic performance of the state is not improving.

The article is organized into seven sections with the first one introducing the need for state-level reforms and outlines the structure of the Punjab economy. Section II provides an overview of the institutional framework for reforms in Punjab. Sections III, IV and V discuss the status of public enterprises, fiscal and industrial reforms in the state. Section VI evaluates the reform process, and is followed by conclusions and suggestions in the final section.

ECONOMY OF PUNJAB

Punjab was one of the fastest growing states of India in the 1970s and the 1980s. The data (GOP, 1992, 1994, 2009) show that when the average Annual Compound Growth Rate (ACGR) of the Gross State Income in India was 4.08 per cent in 1985-86, it was 7.88 per cent in Punjab; when it was 1.20 per cent in India in 1991-92, Gross State Income in Punjab grew at 5.09 per cent. But, when the same for the Indian economy was 9.52 per cent in 2005-06, it was only 4.50 per cent in Punjab, which was less than half of the all India figure. Similarly, in 2007-08 the Gross State Income in India grew at 9.01 percent per annum, while it grew at 6.88 per cent in Punjab.

The average ACGR for various sectors of the economy of Punjab and India also shows similar results. When the growth rate of the primary sector in India in 1985-86 was only 0.87 percent, it was 8.41 per cent in the case of Punjab, and for the secondary sector, the figures were 4.53 per cent and 12.93 per cent respectively for India and Punjab; while the tertiary sectors growth rates were 7.05 per cent and 3.38 per cent for India and Punjab for the same year. The situation remained the same in 1991-92 also, when the primary sector in the country grew at a negative rate, while its growth rate was 5.85 per cent in Punjab. But in 2005-06 the situation reversed and the all – India rate of growth of the primary, secondary and tertiary sectors were 5.75 per cent 10.65 per cent and 10.59 per cent respectively while the same for Punjab were 1.94 per cent, 7.77 per cent and 4.73 per cent. In 2007-08, the annual rates of growth of all the three sectors of the Punjab economy improved, but remained lower than the all- India figures.

The state had the highest per capita income in the country upto 2003-04. The remarkable development record was also manifested in achieving most of the Millennium Development Goals (World Bank, 2004). Most citizens of Punjab have already achieved a level of socio-economic status, that a majority of Indians do not even dream of. The poverty ratio in the state has always been far lower than the all India figures of population below the poverty line (GOP, 2010). In 1973-74, when the population below the poverty line (BPL) in India was 54.93 per cent, it was only 28.08 per cent in Punjab. In 1999-2000 the figures for the country and Punjab respectively were 26.10 per cent and 6.16 per cent and in 2004-05 the same was 21.80 per cent at the all India level and Punjab accounted for only 5.20 per cent of BPL population.

But, Punjab lost its 'numero uno' position gradually, as its pace of growth became slow during the 1990s, and in 2005-06 it was at the third position in terms of per capita income amongst the major Indian states, and in 2007-08 (P) slipped to the fifth position (GOP,2010). The rate of growth of the Punjab economy is much slower than the all-India growth rate. Punjab has grown at a rate of 5.11 percent during the Tenth Five Year Plan, as compared to 7.80 per cent growth of India as a whole. A number of factors are responsible for the slow pace of economic development in Punjab-cross border terrorism affected the state for more than a decade, resulting in not only in deceleration of the growth rate of the economy, but also flight of capital from Punjab; fiscal profligacy of successive governments during the 1990s due to their populist policies; stagnant agriculture, slow pace of industrial development, and last but not the least, the bureaucracy and the polity have been apathetic towards the developmental needs of the state.

Punjab, being a predominantly agricultural economy, has not fully tapped its growth potential in other sectors of the economy. There is tremendous scope for the growth of manufacturing and the services sectors in the state. The government has not made any concerted efforts towards the revival of the primary sector also, though there has been a lot of academic and media focus on the issue.

INSTITUTIONAL FRAMEWORK FOR REFORMS IN PUNJAB

Punjab has a very good record of enacting various acts and legislations as mandated by the Government of India for implementing certain reforms at the state level. The Government of Punjab (GOP) was amongst the first states in the country to constitute a State Finance Commission, as required under Article 243-1 of the Constitution of India as per the 73rd and 74th Constitutional Amendments in 1992. The State Finance Commission is to look into matters relating to state finances, including the transfer of funds from the state government to the Panchayati Raj Institutions (PRIs) and Urban Local Bodies (ULBs), and ways to generate more resources for these institutions. The GOP declared industrial policies in 1992, 1996, 2003 and 2009 to facilitate industrialization of the state and to attract not only domestic private capital, but also foreign capital in tune with national policies. The focus of the policies has been on hassle free investments in Punjab, with various incentives to certain categories of investors like Information Technology (IT) and IT enabled services (ITes), agro-industrial development, power sector reforms, etc. Punjab Information Technology Policy, 2001 is specifically designed to meet the growth requirements of the IT sector in the state. There is a separate Tourism Policy, 2003 meant to tap the tourism potential in Punjab. Punjab State Special Economic Zones (SEZ) Act, 2009 is the sixth SEZ policy at the state level in India. There also exists a Punjab Industrial Facilitation Act, 2005 to further simplify procedures related to industrialization of the state.

The GOP established the Directorate of Disinvestment under the Department of Finance in July 2002 to restructure/privatize the State Level Public Enterprises (SLPEs), and their subsidiaries/promoted companies. Punjab was amongst the first few states to enact the Fiscal Responsibility and Budget Management Act (FRBMA) in October 2003 under the directions of the GoI. The GOP enacted the Punjab Infrastructure Development Act in 2002, and set up the Punjab Infrastructure Regulatory Authority. It has a clear cut policy on Public-Private Partnerships (PPP) in the state. The state also has a Textile Policy, 2006 and Biotech Policy, 2006. Punjab implemented the Value Added Tax (VAT) in 2005, as a part of the tax reform efforts of the GOI.

The GOP set out to carry on power sector reforms, and formed the Punjab State Electricity Regulatory Commission (PSERC) in March 1999 under section 17 of the Electricity Regulatory Commissions Act, 1998, with the objective of rationalization of the electricity tariff, and advising in matters relating to electricity generation, transmission and distribution in the state. Thereafter the Electricity Act , 2003 was enacted, under which the state electricity boards were supposed to bring about massive restructuring/ privatization of the power sector, in order to make them economically viable entities in all the states.

The Punjab Social Development and Governance Reforms Commission was set up to improve the governance and delivery system in the state in January 2009. It is clear that Punjab has an adequate and up to date institutional framework to carry on state-level reforms as needed from time to time, as also directed by the Government of India.

PUBLIC ENTERPRISE REFORMS WITH SPECIAL REFERENCE TO POWER SECTOR REFORMS

The State Public Sector Undertakings (PSUs) consist of companies and statutory corporations of the GOP. Nearly 85 per cent of investment of PSUs is in the power sector, followed by the financial sector (about 7 per cent), while there is only about 3-4 per cent investment in the SLPEs meant to support the agriculture sector. Most of the SLPEs in Punjab have been suffering huge losses and are inefficient, lack transparency and accountability in their working (Sawhney, 1993). Prior to the setting up of the formal framework for disinvestment, it was decided to close down six SLPEs between 1991 and 2001. After the adoption of economic reforms in India, the GOP decided to restructure the

PSUs, and accordingly the State Disinvestment Commission recommended dissolution of nine companies. (Sawhney, 2005). Presently, there are 17 non-working state undertakings and winding up/ closure of the recommended undertakings has not yet been finalized.

As per the Report of the Comptroller and Auditor General of India (2009), during 2004-09, the working public undertakings incurred losses every year except 2004-05. The percentage of turnover of PSUs to the state GDP declined from 15.09 in 2003-04 to 12.04 in 2008-09. The losses of SLPEs are mainly on account of deficiencies in financial management, planning, implementation of projects, running their operations unprofessionally, and lack of monitoring. Most of these losses are controllable, and there is huge avoidable expenditure incurred by these organizations. The return on capital employed has been extremely low in their case, being as low as 0.96 per cent in 2008-09. There are huge accumulated losses, very high debt and interest payments.

The GOP is aware of the serious financial burden of the SLPEs on the public exchequer, but there is absolutely apathy towards taking any concrete steps to divest these loss making undertakings. Most of the undertakings are not only running in perpetual losses, but do not adhere to sound accounting practices as per their respective Acts. They neither finalise their accounts annually within the stipulated period, nor present them for auditing, and thereafter table in the State Legislature. In some cases, the accounts are running into arrears for more than five years. This prevents scrutiny of the working of these organizations. Delay in finalization of the accounts can lead to gross misappropriation of funds and misuse of public money, apart from the provisions of the Companies Act,1956. Thus the SLPEs are a source of major fiscal burden on the state exchequer.

Power sector reforms: Nearly 85 per cent of the public sector investment in Punjab is in the power sector, i.e. the Punjab State Electricity Board (PSEB), which has been running into huge losses over the years due to mismanagement, over-staffing, heavy transmission and distribution losses, unviable electricity tariffs and free power to the agricultural sector. The GOP signed a Memorandum of Understanding with the Union Ministry of Power, for implementation of power sector reforms with identified milestones. The PSEB was to be unbundled into three separate companies for transmission, distribution and generation of electricity in the state as per the Electricity Act, 2003. The Union Government gave a specific time frame to each state to unbundle the power utilities under the Act.

The GOP should have unbundled PSEB, after carefully creating an awareness amongst all the stakeholders regarding its impact, and boldly implemented it by putting all the institutions in place at the earliest; which included the withdrawal of electricity subsidy to certain classes of consumers in the state. Instead, it chose the path of procrastination and kept on postponing the inevitable, in order to retain the populist policy of free power to farmers as well as relenting under trade union pressure. It sought 13 extensions from the Union Government on one pretext or another. Thereafter in April 2010, the Punjab Cabinet decided to corporatise PSEB by creating two separate companies – Punjab State Transmission Corporation Limited (TRANSCO) to look after transmission, and Punjab State Power Corporation Ltd. (POWERCOM) to manage generation and distribution of power in the state. However, both the companies are fully owned and managed by the government and also the staff and their service conditions continue to be the same as PSEB, only they are distributed amongst two new organizations. Tariff continues to be determined by PSERC as in the past, and all the subsidies to different sections of consumers, including farmers continue as before. So far it seems that this structural change in the power sector has been brought about merely to fulfill the obligations laid out in the Electricity Act, 2003 and has not resulted in any radical power sector reforms.

FISCAL REFORMS

Fiscal reforms form a very important part of any reform programme, and enable a government to implement development-oriented policies more effectively. The most important factor responsible for the declining economic performance of Punjab is its gross fiscal mismanagement.

Punjab has been under fiscal stress since the mid-1980s, when it became a revenue deficit state. Punjab had the dubious distinction of being among the states with the highest fiscal deficit in the beginning of the reform period in the country. Militancy, that lasted for over a decade in the state, was one of the major causes of its poor fiscal condition, but was not the only reason. The *White Paper on State Finances* (2002) brings out the factors that adversely impacted the state's fiscal situation, which include the ever increasing burden of committed expenditure – wages, salaries, pensions, interest payments on mounting public debt, power subsidies, loss making public undertakings and slow growth of revenue. Populism undermines the capacity of the government to raise resources and improve the productivity of revenue. Low irrigation charges, abolition of octroi and uneconomic transport fares, added to the burden on the state exchequer, and resulted in further decline in investment on health, education and other social services. The populist policies of the state have resulted in too much indebtedness over the years. The GOP has taken all institutional and sectoral measures suggested by the GOI, the Reserve Bank of India and other agencies to attain fiscal balances and restore macro-economic stability in state finances. An evaluation of the fiscal reform programme of the state reveals, that the Government of Punjab has not adhered to the recommendations of most of the committees and commissions and the financial targets laid down in various documents have rarely been achieved

(Sawhney, 2005). Gross Fiscal Deficit as a proportion of Gross State Domestic Product(GSDP)was 3.1 for the average of 2005-08 and 4.5 for 2008-09(RE) (RBI, 2010), whereas it should not be greater than 3 percent as per the FRBMA. The revenue deficit as percentage of GSDP was 2.5 in 2008-09(RE), the second highest in the country, despite the receipt of Non-plan Revenue Deficit Grant from the GOI from 2005 to 2008 (ICRA,2010). It is notable that on one account, Punjab has met the FRBMA target ,i.e., debt to GSDP ratio which was 43.2 as the average for 2005-08 declined to 40 percent for 2008-09 (RE) ;though the time frame of this target has not been adhered to, as it was supposed to be achieved by 31 March,2007. In short, it may be said that there are serious fiscal imbalances in Punjab despite various reform measures spelt out by the government.

INDUSTRIAL AND INFRASTRUCTURE REFORMS

In line with the GOI , the state governments in the country started drafting new policies to facilitate industrialization under the liberalized and globalized regime. Accordingly, GOP announced its first post-reform industrial policy in 1992 followed by another in 1996, 2003 and the latest being the policy of 2009. Each of these policies brought out , more or less, the same set of strategies for industrial development of the state. All the policies emphasized facilitating the setting up of industries through single window clearances, encouraging foreign direct investment, attracting private domestic investment by offering better incentives vis-à-vis neighbouring states, including fiscal sops and easier land acquisition, etc. The latest policy of 2009, which is based on a review of Punjab's industrial scenario by the United Nations Industrial Development Organization (UNIDO, 2008), is no different from the earlier policies. It does not offer anything which has not earlier been institutionalized through certain organizations, policies, acts and legislations in the state. Punjab has a separate document for every provision made for facilitating industrial development of the state in the new policy.

The key for a high rate of industrial and economic growth is well- developed infrastructure. Budgetary resources are inadequate to Provide the requisite investments to ensure sustainable infrastructure development in Punjab. The punjab Infrastructure Development Board (PIDB) is the nodal agency for facilitating private investment in infrastructure across different sectors - roads and highways, urban infrastructure, industrial infrastructure, electricity, health and education. PIDB is funded through the Punjab Infrastructure Development Fund. The Punjab Infrastructure Initiative Fund (PIIF) has been created to finance project development through the public private partnership (PPP). The state is in dire need of both rural and urban development, airports, good roads and uninterrupted power supply.

AN EVALUATION OF THE REFORMS IN PUNJAB

 As observed in the preceding sections of this article, Punjab has all the legislations, rules and regulations for the development of different sectors of the state. What is glaringly missing in the entire institutional framework, is a comprehensive policy for the revival of agriculture in Punjab. No official document, except the annual budget speeches, spells out a road an map for all-inclusive growth strategy of the state. The present article has not dealt with certain socio-economic indicators reflecting poor gender ratio, lack of proper civic amenities, as well as the dire necessity for health and education reforms in the state. The entire success of the policy depends on its implementation, i.e. the strategy, seriousness and the delivery system. Mere enactment of such policies has no meaning. Various concessions and subsidies offered to attract industry can only be granted, if the financial health of the state allows it. Presently, such is not the case. Also, a prerequisite for the rapid and effective development of any sector, hinges on good infrastructure including assured power availability. Punjab is not able to meet these conditions at present. The state does not offer an investor-friendly environment, and so has not been able to attract any major domestic or foreign industrial/service sector project, except a joint venture refinery between Hindustan Petroleum Corporation Ltd. (HPCL) and Mittal Energy Investments Pte. Ltd., Singapore, known as HMEL. There is hardly any simplification of procedures for setting up a business in Punjab, on the contrary, there are too many bureaucratic hurdles and corruption is rampant in the state.

It is not the content of the industrial policy in Punjab that matters, but the capability of its polity and bureaucracy to implement not only this policy, but several other commitments made to the people of Punjab, to improve the quality of their lives, as also arrest deceleration of the state economy. This requires an enabling environment, including investments in technological and organizational capabilities of the state. The much talked about e-governance, put to effective use by other states, is far from being attempted in Punjab. Accountability of administrative performance is necessary for all the stakeholders, including the corporate sector, the civil society and the non-government organizations. There is a huge potential for industrial and service sector growth, particularly, agro-industrial development in Punjab, if the GOP implements certain decisions which may not be populist and may seem harsh in the short run, but will accelerate the pace of growth of the economy of Punjab and will confer political dividends in the long run.

Although the Punjab government has formulated various policies for encouraging industrialization of the state, yet there are certain decisions which the government takes outside the formal institutional framework. A case in point is that of the issue of concessions to HMEL. After the final negotiations of the promoters with the GOP in 2005 regarding concessions, now nearing completion, the company is asking for further concessions and the GOP is seriously considering this proposal which is not a prudent fiscal step. Renegotiation undermines the credibility of the government and erodes confidence of the people. There should be a definite, well-defined, objective and transparent criterion laid down in industrial policy, listing concessions and subsidies for promoting industrialization. There should not be any tinkering in the already framed strategy. Doling out ad-hoc concessions under the influence of powerful industrialists or lobbies, is bound to raise issues about the credibility and transparency of the government.

Punjab's record in infrastructure development is far from satisfactory. Most of the agri-infrastructure created in the state during the period of the Green Revolution, i.e. during the 1970s and 1980s, has neither been upgraded nor supplemented. Due to the weak fiscal position of the state, as well as the apathy of the government, many vital sectors of the economy have remained neglected, e.g. education and health. Punjab failed to avail funds from the central government/Planning Commission for several social welfare/ education/health and infrastructure development schemes. The review carried out by the Planning Commission (2009) reveals that during the Tenth Five Year Plan, the utilization of funds for centrally sponsored schemes was only 54.13 per cent in Punjab. The major factor adversely impacting the schemes was non-release of the share of the state which was only 22 per cent. In 2009-10, there was only 36.81 per cent achievement against the Annual Work Plan in Sarva Siksha Abhiyan, and under the National Rural Health Mission there was only 37 per cent utilization of the available funds. In the case of certain schemes, there has been absolutely no utilization of funds. There is gross under utilization of funds under all the central schemes in Punjab, which leads not only to non-creation of socio-economic infrastructure in the state, but also available funds are wasted at a time when the state is starved of developmental resources.

Governance reforms are central for the successful implementation of the Jawaharlal Nehru National Urban Renewal Mission (JNNURM). The main objective of the implementation of reforms under JNNURM is to provide an enabling environment for the growth of our cities, by enhancing effective urban service delivery, land management, financial management and stakeholder participation in local governance. The withdrawal of property tax in Punjab is in contravention of the spirit of JNNURM.

CONCLUSION

The governments in Punjab, since the mid-1990s, have been pursuing populist policies in the expectation of creating vote banks and returning to power, but the reality has been to the contrary, i.e., the same political party in the state has not returned to power for two consecutive terms.

The following reforms are urgently needed in Punjab, if economic deceleration in the state is to be seriously arrested:

1. Agriculture development
   - A renewed thrust is required for putting agriculture back on the growth path, with special emphasis on making agriculture more remunerative.
   - Special efforts have to be made for creating new and modern agri-infrastructure, maintenance, modernization and upgradation of existing facilities as per contemporary requirements, wherever diversification out of wheat-paddy has taken place.
   - An area which requires a fresh impetus through public investment is agricultural research and development, which was the harbinger of growth and success of the Green Revolution in the mid-1960s and 1970s in Punjab. The government seems to have lost focus on this account; this needs to be pursued with renewed zeal and vigour.
   - A clear cut land acquisition policy, along with a framework for the rehabilitation of the uprooted farmers is urgently required.

2. Fiscal responsibility is a prerequisite for arresting further deterioration in the economy of Punjab, and putting it back on the path of development:
   - Reduction and maintenance of fiscal deficit and debt to GSDP ratios as per the FRBMA, 2003 is imperative.
   - Improving the composition of public expenditures, by reducing the share spent on wages, pensions, interest payments, agricultural subsidies, notably power subsidy.
   - Utilizing funds allocated under centrally sponsored schemes effectively.
   - Encouraging local governments to mobilize resources as well as adhering to the Constitutional commitment of devolution of funds to the ULBs and PRIs.

3. Conducive investment climate for industry and the services sectors:
   - Implementing provisions for the efficient growth of the industrial and services sectors as per various state policies, and facilitation acts enacted from time to time.
   - Encouraging the growth of both the sectors by strengthening the infrastructure, and improving the performance of the civil services and quality of service delivery

by improving public access to information, strengthening accountability, bringing about transparency and reducing political interference.

- Delivery of public services needs to be strengthened with a focus on health, education, rural and urban development.

- Restricting unplanned urbanization, and regulating urban development through the PPP mode and use of precious public resources for inclusive growth.

- Capacity building of the state administration for the implementation of various central and state schemes is very essential.

A perusal of the economic reform programme in Punjab, suggests that the governments of the state, since the mid-1990s, have been indulging in competitive politics and have paid no heed to the developmental needs of the state. It is only a comprehensive multi-sectoral development policy, coupled with effective governance and service delivery, which can arrest the deteriorating economic condition of the state. Populist policies, destroying the roots of development, cannot be sustained in the long run. It has been proposed by Bhagwati and Panagariya (2004), that economic performance has become an important determinant of voter behaviour in recent years. This explains the reason for anti-incumbency to be a prominent feature of election outcomes. Gupta and Panagariya (2010) have brought out a very strong relationship between growth performance and election outcomes. Superior growth performance is positively associated with good governance and law and order.

A state policy can be termed as "public policy" only if it promotes public interest. The interest of the masses must be protected, and the poor be given priority in the allocation of public resources. If such policies create disproportionate gains for one section of society at the cost of others, these can create instability in the system. Populist policies create wider social and economic disparities than they bridge. Such policies are neither economically sound nor benefit the people for whom they are meant (subsidized farm outputs, including free power, have rarely benefited the small and marginal farmers); rather, they weaken the system if pursued indiscriminately over a long period of time.

It is worth noting that the Punjab government set up the Punjab Social Development and Governance Reforms Commission to suggest ways and means to improve governance and delivery systems of various public services in the state. This amounts to an admission by the government, that there are serious flaws in the delivery systems, policy implementation and the quality of governance. However, the Commission has submitted three reports to the GOP, but no action has been initiated on any of the recommendations so far, rather the term of the Commission has been extended by one more year. This further reflects the apathy of the government towards the urgency of improving the quality of administration in Punjab to put it back on the path to economic recovery.

REFERENCES

[1] Ahluwalia, M.S. (2001). *State Level Performance Under Economic Reforms in India.* SCID Working Paper 96: Center for Research on Economic Development and Policy Reform, Stanford University.

[2] Ahluwalia, I.J., Chaudhri,S. and Sidhu,S. (2008). *Punjab Industrial Review.* United Nations Industrial Development Organization. Online. Available at:http://www.unido.org/fileadmin/user_media/Publications/Pub_free/Punjab_industrial_review.pdf

[3] Allebaut, John J. (2005). Taking Reforms to India's States. Online. Available at:http://www.cipe.org/publications/ert/e23/E23_05.pdf

[4] Bhagwati, J. and Panagariya, A. (2004). Great Expectations. *Wall Street Journal.* May24.

[5] Ghosh, A., Roy,J and Nayar, A. (2010). *Fiscal Consolidation: Challenges for Indian States.*Online. Available at: www.icra.org

[5] Government of Punjab (2002). *White Paper on the State's Finances.* Chandigarh: Department of Finance.

[6] Government of Punjab (1992, 1994, 2009). *Statistical Abstract of Punjab.* Chandigarh: Economic and Statistical Organisation.

[7] Government of Punjab. (2009) *Report of the Comptroller and Auditor General of India (Commercial).* Chandigarh : Comptroller and Auditor General of India.

[8] Government of Punjab. (2010). *Economic Survey.* Chandigarh: Economic and Statistical Organisation.

[9] Gupta,P and Panagariya, A. (2010). *India: Election Outcomes and Economic Performance.* Paper presented at Conference on India: Economic Policies and Outcomes. School of International and Public Affairs, Columbia University.

[10] Howes, S, Lahiri, A and Stern, N (ed.). (2003). *State Level Reforms in India: Towards More Effective Government.* .New Delhi: Macmillan India Ltd.

[11] Nambiar, ACK. (2007). State Level Fiscal Reform in India: Strategy and its Implications. Online. Available at: http://ideas.repec.org/s/icf/icfjpf.html

[12] Nambiar,ACK. (2010). Fiscal Performance of States: An Alternative Approach to Measurement. Online. Available at: http://ideas.repec.org/s/icf/icfjpf.html

[13] Planning Commission. (2009). *Note on Review/Inspection of Flagship/Other Important Centrally Sponsored Schemes in State of Punjab.* Online. Available at: http://planningcommission.gov.in/reports/advstates/advtostate/punjab_visit.pdf

[14] Sawhney, U. (1993). Public Enterprise in a Predominantly Agricultural Economy : A Case Study of Punjab. Unpublished Thesis , Punjabi University, Patiala.

[15] Sawhney, U. (2005). *Fiscal Reforms at the Sub-national Level: The Case of Punjab.* NIPFP Working Paper 26: National Institute of Public Finance and Policy, New Delhi.

[16] World Bank, (2004). *Resuming Punjab's Prosperity:The Oppurtunities and Challenges Ahead.* New Delhi: World Bank.

[17] World Bank. (2005). *State Level Fiscal Reforms in India: Progress and Prospects*, New Delhi: Macmillan India Ltd.

Role of Microfinance on the Economic Status of Self-employed Women in India

Arvind Kumar and V. Ravi[1]

Department of Statistics, LSR College, New Delhi
[1]Department of Commerce, LSR College, New Delhi

ABSTRACT

Micro Finance has long been recognized as the key for economic growth. The role of micro finance, especially for Self-Employed Women (SEW) entrepreneurs who successfully exploit industrial and commercial opportunities on a small scale, cannot be under estimated. Self-employed women help in enhancing economic growth, because they have a better chance to carry out innovations, and new means of production. In the olden days, Indian women were mainly rendering services to the family members, particularly to the husband and children, and hence were not allowed to venture out for an earning income. In most areas, they were not even allowed to go for higher education. India being a country with 70 per cent of its population belonging to rural sector, depends on agriculture and allied activities, and therefore faces many problems to generate income for sustaining the rural masses.

Due to various social and traditional reasons, women started to generate incomes. At present, women contribute much for the development of all sectors of the country. Employment gives economic status to women. Economic status increases social status and thereby empowerment. By keeping this in view, all governments try to improve the status of women in all possible ways. Self-employed groups of women are considered as the main channel for generating income for the women in all areas, particularly in the rural and semi-urban areas. The growth of SEW is evidence of the fact that women are coming out of their shells, shunning their second class citizen status, and are using their potential and talents for individual and societal benefits. In this context, Self-employed Women are improving the socio-economic status of other women.

Keywords: SEW: Self-employed Women, Women Empowerment, Socio-economic Status.

INTRODUCTION

Self-employment is the individual pursuit of capitalism. To be self-employed, an individual should be highly skilled in a trade, or have a niche product, or perform service for their local community. With the creation of the Internet, the ability of an individual to become self-employed has increased dramatically. The amount of money spent on self-help, self-improvement and training materials has reached billions in the past decade.

Self-employed people can also be referred to as a person who works for himself/herself instead of an employer, but drawing income from a trade or business that they operate personally.

To be self-employed, is not the same as being a business owner: A business owner is not required to be hands-on with the day-to-day operations of his or her company, while a self-employed person has to have a very hands-on approach in order to survive.

MICROFINANCE IN INDIA

The irrepressible desire and inherent capacity of the poor to improve their living standards, is considered as the foundation for the concept of micro finance, propelled by the demonstrative success of the Bangladesh *Grameen* Experiment. **Microfinance** is acknowledged as an effective channel to take the poor into a new domain of economic empowerment. The micro finance movement assumed global advocacy through the **Microcredit** Summit held in February 1997 in Washington. The summit representing 1500 institutions and 137 countries is a landmark, in the collective crusade against poverty undertaken by the developed and developing countries together. The **Microcredit** Summit launched a campaign to reach 100 million of the worlds poorest families. **Microfinance** is referred as providing credit for self employment, financial and other business services, including savings and technical assistance.

In India SEW is an integral part of the National Bank for Agriculture and Rural Development (NABARD) and other financial institutions.

RESEARCH PROBLEM

In today's environment, we find that women are flourishing in every field and discipline. Taking this as a motivation, rural poor women were stimulated and associated for mutual help. This initiated a process where they started to improve their status, standards of living and personality. No more are women considered to be dependent. They are finding their own ways of generating income. They not only improve themselves, but they also associate other poor women with them and jointly work to improve everyone's status.

In order to create awareness among the women, and to give a detailed analytical performance of micro finance, the researcher has attempted to analyze the impact of micro finance for SEW in India.

OBJECTIVES OF THE STUDY

The objectives of the study are the following:

1. To study the socio-economic conditions of self-employed women.
2. To measure the impact of micro finance on the group of self employed women in India.

This research study will help women to strengthen their economic activities, to create positive linkages, and to support in accessing raw materials, skill training, marketing opportunities and credit needs. The present study is aimed at analyzing the impact of micro finance in terms of the economic status of the SEW.

RESEARCH METHODOLOGY

The present study is based on both primary and secondary data. The main source of the primary data is from SEW. Interviews have been used for collecting information relating to the socio-economic conditions, and the impact of micro finance from SEW. The data thus collected were categorized and posted in the master table for further processing. The collected data was analyzed through simple descriptive statistics for the 'F' test. The extent and variation of economic status achieved by the members was measured by a scale and analysis on the basis of the scores of the components.

SAMPLING

The present study proposes to cover SEW in India. Data was collected by interviewing a total of 200 women across various states in India. The respective sample distribution is as follows:

Table 1

State	SEW
Uttar Pradesh	50
Madhya Pradesh	25
Rajasthan	25
Delhi	60
Haryana	40
TOTAL	200

ANALYSIS

An attempt was made by the researcher to present the socio-economic conditions of SEW in India. Sample members were divided into three categories, based on their respective scores. The distribution of respondents according to their levels of economic status is shown in Table 2.

AGE GROUP AND ECONOMIC STATUS

The sample respondents were grouped into three age groups. Sample SEW members in the age group up to 30 years were classified as *young*, those between 31 and 50 years as *middle-aged* and those above 50 years as *old*. Table 2 reveals the relationship between age and economic status. In order to determine the association between the age group of the respondents and their economic status, Chi-square test was applied.

Table 2: Age Group * Socio-Economic Status Cross tabulation

			Socio-economic Status			Total
			Low	Medium	High	
Age Group	Young	Count	9	34	4	47
		% within Socio-economic Status	32.1%	23.9%	13.3%	23.5%
	Middle-Aged	Count	12	87	18	117
		% within Socio-economic Status	42.9%	61.3%	60.0%	58.5%
	Old	Count	7	21	8	36
		% within Socio-economic Status	25.0%	14.8%	26.7%	18.0%
Total		Count	28	142	30	200
		% within Socio-economic Status	100.0%	100.0%	100.0%	100.0%

We may conclude (at 5 percent level of significance) on the basis of the chi-square test, that the age-group has no association with the socio-economic status of the individual (p-value = 0.170 < 0.05).

AREA OF RESIDENCE AND ECONOMIC STATUS

On applying the chi-square test, we obtained a p-value of 0.000 which implies that there is a strong association between the area of residence and the socio-economic status. As we can see, that out of the 42 rural respondents, 54.8 per cent belong to the low

Table 3: Area of Residence * Socio-economic Status Cross tabulation

			Socio-economic Status			
			Low	Medium	High	Total
Area of Residence	Rural	Count	23	18	1	42
		% within Area of Residence	54.8%	42.9%	2.4%	100.0%
	Semi-Urban	Count	4	84	2	90
		% within Area of Residence	4.4%	93.3%	2.2%	100.0%
	Urban	Count	1	40	27	68
		% within Area of Residence	1.5%	58.8%	39.7%	100.0%
Total		Count	28	142	30	200
		% within Area of Residence	14.0%	71.0%	15.0%	100.0%

economic status. Similarly, of the 90 semi-urban respondents, 93.3 per cent belong to medium and of the 68 urban respondents, 39.7 per cent belong to the high economic status. Hence, we note, that as the area of residence changes from rural to urban, the socio-economic status moves from lower to higher grades.

MARITAL STATUS AND ECONOMIC STATUS

Married men and women have more responsibilities. An attempt was made to find whether the level of economic status varies with the marital status of respondents. Chi-square test between socio-economic status and marital status yields a p-value of 0.000, which confirms our earlier beliefs that both are associated.

Table 4: Marital Status * Socio-economic Status Cross tabulation

			Socio-economic Status			
			Low	Medium	High	Total
Marital Status	Married	Count	1	119	17	137
		% within Marital Status	.7%	86.9%	12.4%	100.0%
	Unmarried	Count	7	10	11	28
		% within Marital Status	25.0%	35.7%	39.3%	100.0%
	Divorced	Count	20	13	2	35
		% within Marital Status	57.1%	37.1%	5.7%	100.0%
Total		Count	28	142	30	200
		% within Marital Status	14.0%	71.0%	15.0%	100.0%

Of the 137 married respondents, 99.3 per cent (86.9+12.4) have their economic status above medium. Also of the 28 unmarried respondents 75 per cent (35.7+39.3) have their economic status as medium or high. However, of the 35 divorced respondents, 57.1 per cent belong to the low economic status.

CASTE AND ECONOMIC STATUS

Social status of members is considered for assessing the level of economic status. An attempt was made to analyse whether economic status varies between the various categories (in terms of caste) of members. The chi-square test for association gives a p-value of 0.000 and hence, caste and economic status are associated. We observe that the SC/ST have a low to medium economic status, whereas OBC and general candidates have medium to high economic status.

Table 5: Caste * Socio-economic Status Cross tabulation

			Socio-economic Status			
			Low	Medium	High	Total
Caste	SC/ST	Count	18	20	1	39
		% within Caste	46.2%	51.3%	2.6%	100.0%
	OBC	Count	2	4	4	10
		% within Caste	20.0%	40.0%	40.0%	100.0%
	General	Count	8	118	25	151
		% within Caste	5.3%	78.1%	16.6%	100.0%
Total		Count	28	142	30	200
		% within Caste	14.0%	71.0%	15.0%	100.0%

Source: Primary Data

EDUCATION AND ECONOMIC STATUS

Educated members might be aware of the ways and means of utilizing micro finance. For this, the sample members were classified according to their level of education as shown in Table 6. Of the 43 illiterate respondents, 27 respondents 90.7 percent (41.9+48.8) had their economic status as either low or medium. Out of 24 respondents with primary education and 45 with secondary education, 75 percent and 71.1 percent of respondents had medium economic status respectively. Finally, out of 88 respondents with higher than secondary education, 80.7 percent respondents have medium whereas 15 percent have high economic status. The p-value for the chi-square test was found to be highly significant.

Table 6: Education * Socio-Ecomsee, Status Crosstabulation

| | | | Socio-economic Status | | | |
			Low	Medium	High	Total
Education	Illiterate	Count	18	21	4	43
		% within Education	41.9%	48.8%	9.3%	100.0%
	Primary	Count	3	18	3	24
		% within Education	12.5%	75.0%	12.5%	100.0%
	Secondary	Count	4	32	9	45
		% within Education	8.9%	71.1%	20.0%	100.0%
	Higher than Secondary	Count	3	71	14	88
		% within Education	3.4%	80.7%	15.9%	100.0%
Total		Count	28	142	30	200
		% within Education	14.0%	71.0%	15.0%	100.0%

AWARENESS OF MICRO FINANCE AND ECONOMIC STATUS

Awareness regarding various activities related to SEW and micro finance, enables members to understand their responsibilities and application of such provisions. For this purpose, the sample respondents were classified into two groups, namely those who were aware and unaware of the SEW. In order to find out the association between awareness of the respondents and their economic status, the chi-square test was applied, and found to be highly significant.

Table 7: Awareness * Socio-economic Status Cross tabulation

| | | | Socio-economic Status | | | |
			Low	Medium	High	Total
Awareness	Aware	Count	7	104	29	140
		% within Socio-Economic Status	25.0%	73.2%	96.7%	70.0%
	Unaware	Count	21	38	1	60
		% within Socio-Economic Status	75.0%	26.8%	3.3%	30.0%
Total		Count	28	142	30	200
		% within Socio-Economic Status	100.0%	100.0%	100.0%	100.0%

Of the 28 respondents belonging to the low economic status, 75 per cent were unaware of the SEW. Also out of 142 and 30 respondents belonging to medium and high economic status, 73.2 per cent and 96.7 per cent respectively were aware of SEW. This clearly illustrates the role of SEW and its awareness as major factors, determining the economic status of the individual.

RECOMMENDATIONS

In the light of the findings made in this study, the following recommendations are suggested to improve the function of micro finance for self employed women.

GENERAL RECOMMENDATIONS

1. There should public private partnerships for SEW. Networking of this group is essential for sharing and resolving common problems. Exposure visits to relatively successful group ventures of other SEWs can be organized to share knowledge, experience and expertise. Failures in many organizations are due to ineffective management, and SEW are not free from that. Simple management techniques and applications can be taught to them with the help of management faculties and experts.

2. Micro finance should be used to meet current demands of self-employed women, irrespective of the field of employment. This will enable them to identify activities for economic betterment

3. Training in book-keeping, accounts, fund management, using TALLY and other financial matters related to self-employment are essential, to make them competent enough to deal with the increasing volume of transactions.

4. Most of the SEWs procure their raw materials locally for production. When there are shortages or non-availability of raw materials, agencies like cooperative agricultural societies and marketing societies should come forward to help SEW. These agencies may create a link with the SEWs.

5. Surveys of SEW must be conducted every year in order to identify the eligible beneficiaries of micro finance, and to allocate funds according to the felt needs of the people.

6. Voluntary organizations operating in rural areas should be encouraged to participate in the effective implementation of the programme. The programme may provide separate funds for the projects to be taken up by such organizations.

RECOMMENDATIONS FOR BANKS

1. Commercial banks should give wider publicity on the availability of credit facilities that can be offered to the SEW. Bank officials can give more information about the

procedures in getting loans, utilization of loan amount repayment and other related information in securing credit. Simple procedures and the right encouragement from bank officials may enable women to take advantage.

2. In any credit facility, loan repayment is important. SEW are funded mainly by financial agencies. Such agencies should guide them about repayments. Mounting over-dues are the biggest problem for cooperatives, and this should not happen in the case of SEWS.

RECOMMENDATION FOR THE GOVERNMENT

1. The government should come forward to provide minimum entrepreneurship program through the district industries centers. Programmes can be design in consultation with industry consultants which may lead to capacity building of the SEW.

2. Government should organize micro credit camps and credit cum-recovery camps to facilitate early completion of the formalities, required for sanctioning loans and to avoid hardship to the beneficiaries.

3. The government, NGOs and financial agencies should help SEWs in selecting the projects or the ventures. Depending on local conditions, availability of raw materials and other factors, they can advice SEW to select feasible and profitable ventures. Ideas of SEW should be scrutinized with the help of management experts, before the venture is finalized. Errors in selecting projects may make for closure, as a result the time and money put in the project could be wasted. Hence, right directions may enable the SEWs to select the right ventures.

4. Government should make rural people to realize that SEWs are the main medium for rural employment generation, Encouragement and support by the government will solve the problem of rural unemployment. Everyone has entrepreneurial abilityes and India needs rural entrepreneurs to solve employment problems. This paves the way for women empowerment in India.

CONCLUSIONS

The researchers present this study in the fervent hope that this will draw the attention of the authorities, departments and organizations concerned with micro finance and SEW on various issues, in respect of the development of women empowerment. Through this study, we have found that parameters like area of residence, marital status, caste, education and awareness have a major affect on the socio-economic status of women. The factors leading to medium and high socio-economic status are found to be urban area of residence, married persons, general and OBC castes, secondary and higher education and awareness of SEW.

In all, there should be proper coordination and cohesive efforts by various agencies, viz., government, voluntary organizations, commercial banks, etc., to alleviate the socio-economic status of self employed women in India.

REFERENCES

[1] Desai, Bhupat M. and Namboodiri N.V, (1996). "Whither Rural Financial Institutions", *Economic and Political Weekly, Mumbai*, August 3, Vol. 31, No. 31, pp. 2341-2342.

[2] Jesselyn, Mary (2004) "The Formal Institutional Framework of Entrepreneurship In The Philippines: Lessons for Developing Countries", *The Journal of Entrepreneurship*, Vol. 13(2), pp. 185-203.

[3] Kaladhar, K. (1997) "Micro Finance in India: Design, Structure and Governance", *Economic and Political Weekly*, Mumbai, Vol. 32, No. 42, October 2007, pp. 3512-3513.

[4] Matlay, Harry (2006) "Researching Entrepreneurship and Education", Emerald Group Publishing The Emerald Publishing Group are a primary publisher of management and business journals. Based in the UK, they operate worldwide with offices in Malaysia, Japan, China, India and the United States. Ltd., Vol. 48 (8/ 9), pp. 704-718.

[5] Naila Kabeer, "Is Microfinance a 'Magic Bullet' for Women's Empowerment? Analysis of Findings from South Asia", *Economic and Political Weekly*, Mumbai, October 2006, p. 2642.

[6] Panda S. K., "Micro Finance in Economic Empowerment of Weaker Sections", *Yojana*, New Delhi, March 2003, Vol. 47, No.3, p. 19.

[7] Revathi K. "Micro Finance: A Tool for Poverty Alleviation", *Facts For You*, New Delhi, June 2007, p. 16.

[8] Rinkal, Divya and Sneha (2004). "Women Entrepreneurs—Critical Issues." Proceedings of the 11th Summer Camp on "Entrepreneurial Stimulation for Children from May 2-7, 2004.

[9] Srinivasa Rao K., "Microfinance: A Tool for Poverty Alleviation and Women Empowerment", *Facts for You*, New Delhi, January 2007, p. 32.

URL

[1] http.//www.gatwayofmicrofinancne.com
[2] http://www.nen.org
[3] http.//www.sewa.org

Functions of Panchayati Raj Institutions at a Glance

H.R. Bangia

NIPCCD IIPA, Haryana Regional Branch

I must confess that I have not been able to follow the proceedings of the Constituent Assembly... (the correspondence) says that there is no mention or direction about village panchayats and decentralization in the foreshadowed constitution. It is certainly an omission calling for immediate attention if our independence is to reflect the people's voice. The greater the power of the panchayats, the better for the people...

Gandhi

Harijan

Unless there is reform in one-self, one should not expect reform in self-governance

– H.R. Bangia

INTRODUCTION

With Effect from 24, April, 1993, the Constitution of India contains a new Chapter, Part IX titled "The Panchayats", the term "Panchayat" being defined by Article 243(D) as "an institution (by whatever name called) of self-government... for the rural areas," the term "rural areas" being nowhere further defined except derivatively in Article 243 (G), wherein the enabling provision empowers the Governor to specify a "village" by public notification through the 73rd Constitutional Amendment and with the 74th Amendment, has mandated the establishment of the District Planning Committee (DPC) for consolidating plans prepared by panchayats and municipalities in the district into the draft district plan.[1]

An institutional network of "Panchayats" has been, thus mandated into existence by the Articles 243, 243A and 243B of the Constitution of India, which explicitly declare such institutions to be "institutions of self-government" – a status and/or nomenclature denied even to the union government (Part II) and state governments (Part III). What are the constitutional implications of this form of institutionalization of panchayats, or more explicitly, what specific benefits/costs are attached to the "panchayats" constitutional zed as "institutions of self-government"? The Eleventh Plan, which has identified inclusive growth as its core vision, seeks to "substantially empower and use PRIs as the primary means of delivery of essential services that are critical for inclusive growth."

The Plan asserts that 'it is absolutely critical for the inclusiveness of our growth process that these large numbers of elected representatives of PRIs are fully involved in planning, implementing and supervising the delivery of essential public services.

The Seventy-third Amendment provides constitutional sanction for state legislations, giving a new status to Panchayati Raj. Further, it has imparted a kind of permanency to the PRIs, and has deepened the reach of decentralised polity through a multi-level structure of self-government. Panchayati Raj bodies have been empowered to have core developmental functions, and exercise conduct of business in better participatory processes to strengthen their stand. Funds in rural areas can be utilised in terms of local relevance and specificities. A number of poverty alleviation programmes can be streamlined for the benefit of the needs of the local people.

A detailed road map as to how this could be achieved has been elaborated in the Plan document in Chapter 10, to that entitled *Governance* which recognizes decentralization and strengthening of PRIs as a major challenge The establishment of a separate *Ministry of Panchayati Raj in May 2004 at the Centre* is a clear indication of major push to such reforms.[2]

BRIEF HISTORICAL BACKGROUND OF PANCHAYATI RAJ

On 29 January, 1925, Mahatma Gandhi for the first time spoke about Swaraj, Panchayati Raj and Rural Development in Young India in the following words:

> "By Swaraj I mean the Government of India by the consent of the people as ascertained by the largest number of the adult population, male or female, native-born or domiciled, who have contributed by manual labour to the service of the state and who have taken the trouble of having registered their names as voters.... Real Swaraj will come not by the acquisition of authority by a few, but by the acquisition of the capacity by all to resist authority when it is abused. In other words, Swaraj is to be obtained by educating the masses to a sense of their capacity to regulate and control authority."

The system of Panchayati Raj came into existence through a very long process of evolution of the institutional framework for development of rural areas. In 1952, the nationwide community development programmes were introduced, wherein the process of development came to be in the framework of the concept of 'democratic decentralisation.' One of the concepts was that the PRIs at three levels were mere 'agencies' or 'limbs' of the state government, for the execution of development programmes, and of such administrative responsibilities as were given to them by law or government order. The other concept was that the PRIs were each at their level, organs of self-government. With the introduction of the 64th Constitution Amendment Bill in the late 80s, which envisaged a constitutional status for the elected bodies at the lower levels of administration, initiated the beginning of a new strength to the system of Panchayati Raj in India. By and by the process resulted in the passage of the 73rd Constitution Amendment, which is a significant landmark in the area of development planning in India. It provides for the transfer of power centres from the apex of administrative hierarchy to the elected representatives of the people at the grassroot levels, and to provide freedom to the masses to shape their destiny. The difference from the erstwhile development planning and the present one is that it now revolves around the rural masses themselves who are the beneficiaries. In fact, the Constitution of India and the First Five Year Plan eloquently elaborated the vision of India. It has been stressed that the planning will have to be rooted in the aspirations and expectations of the people at the grass-roots levels.

The Act now provides adequate representation for scheduled castes and scheduled tribes and women in the elected bodies at all levels, with an enabling provision for a similar reservations for other backward classes. The other features of this Act are: a fixed tenure of five years; regular elections and mechanisms to ensure appropriate financial allocations to strengthen these bodies. It also includes assignment of functions in respect of: (i) preparation of plans for economic development and social justice, and (ii) implementation of schemes for economic development and social justice. This has prompted all the states to get the respective bills passed within the stipulated time, in order to hold elections and have the PRIs in position. There are, however, variations in allocation of business to the bodies and financial dispensations,which need to be studied to make the PRIs uniform in all the states of India. [3]

AREAS OF PLANNING AT DIFFERENT LEVELS OF PRIs

Article 243G of the Constitution envisages that with regard to matters relating to economic development and social justice, Panchayats should be entrusted with the preparation of plans and implementation of schemes so as to enable them to function as institutions of local self-governance. For meeting these objectives, the state governments are expected to devolve powers, authority, and responsibility on to Panchayats. An illustrative list comprising 29 such subjects has been presented in Annexure 1.

RELEVANCE OF SEATS RESERVED FOR WOMEN, SCs/STs AND OBCs ARTICLE 243(D) PROVIDES:[4]

1. Reservation of seats for
   (a) the scheduled castes; and
   (b) the scheduled tribes, in every Panchayat and the number of seats so reserved shall bear, as nearly as may be, the same proportion to the total number of seats to be filled by direct election in that Panchayat, as the population of the scheduled castes in that Panchayat area, or of the scheduled tribes in that Panchayat area bears to the total population of that area, and such seats may be allotted by rotation to different constituencies in a Panchayat.

2. Not less than one-third of the total number of seats reserved under clause (1) shall be reserved for women belonging to the scheduled castes, or, as the case may be, the scheduled tribes.

3. Not less than one-third (including the number of seats reserved for women belonging to the scheduled castes and the scheduled tribes) of the total number of seats, to be filled by direct election in every Panchayat, shall be reserved for women and such seats may be allotted by rotation to different constituencies in a Panchayat.

4. The office of the Chairpersons in the Panchayat at the village, or any other level, shall be reserved for the scheduled castes, the scheduled tribes, and women in such manner as the Legislature of a state may, by law, provide:

   Provided that the number of offices of Chairpersons reserved for the scheduled castes and scheduled tribes in the Panchayats at each level in any state shall bear, as nearly as may be, the same proportion to the total number of such offices in the Panchayats at each level as the population of the scheduled castes, in the state, or of the scheduled tribes in the state bears to the total population of the state:

   Provided further, that not less than one-third of the total number of offices of Chairpersons in the Panchayats at each level shall be reserved for women:

   Provided also that the number of offices reserved under this clause shall be allotted by rotation to different Panchayats at each level.

5. The reservation of seats under clause (1) and (2) and the reservation of the office of Chairpersons (other than the reservation for women) under clause (4) shall cease to have effect on the expiration of the period specified in Article 334.

6. Nothing in this part shall prevent the Legislature of a state from making any provision for reservation of seats in any Panchayat, or office of Chairpersons in the Panchayats at any level in favour of backward class of citizens.

7. *Amendment to article 243D of the Constitution of India for enhancing reservation for women in Panchayats to 50 per cent:* The Union Cabinet on 27, August, 2009 approved the proposal for moving a Constitutional Amendment Bill for enhancing reservations for women in Panchayats at all tiers from one third to at least 50 per cent. This provision will apply to the total number of seats filled by direct election, offices of Chairpersons and seats and offices of Chairpersons reserved for scheduled castes and scheduled tribes.

In view of the earlier statements and on perusal of the 29 developmental functions, it would show that all the 29 items also apply to the developmental needs of the SCs/STs. The aspirations of this class of people are that they are given due consideration through the elected representatives of the SCs and STs. For example, Item 8 which relates to "minor forest produce" is of special significance for the scheduled tribes, as they are directly involved in the collection of minor forest produce, but they are in this occupation as only wage earners. The aspirations of these people can be fruitful if the elected representatives give a chance to these class of people only, so that the local produce is not handled and managed by other than SCs/STs and weaker sections of society.

REVIEW OF PRIs AND THE ROAD AHEAD

The Panchayati Raj institutions in India last year completed the 50 years since inception. The celebrations were marked by the observance of 2009-10 *As Year of the Gram Sabha*. The number of grassroots institutions was about 2.52 lakhs. In order to enhance the empowerment of women at the grassroots, the *government has already decided to earmark 50 per cent*. This is the greatest experiment in democracy ever undertaken anywhere in the world at any time in history.

The mandate of the Ministry of Panchayati Raj is enshrined in Part IX of the Constitution ("The Panchayats") read with Article 243 ZD of Part IXA, relating to the District Planning Committees and the Eleventh Schedule which sets out a list of 29 matters (as stated in the foregoing paragraphs), which might be considered by state legislatures for devolution to the Panchayats in respect of the planning of economic development and social justice, as well as the implementation of "entrusted" schemes of economic and social development in such a manner, as to ensure that they function as "units of self-government".

CELEBRATION OF 2009 AS THE YEAR OF THE GRAM SABHA

On 2 October, 2009 Panchayati Raj in India completed its golden jubilee. 50 years ago on 2 October, 1959, Pt. Jawaharlal Nehru, the first Prime Minister of India laid the foundations of Panchayati Raj at Naguar in Rajasthan. To mark the occasion, a national convention was organized at Vigyan Bhawan. The occasion was to witness two major announcements – the renaming of the National Rural Employment Guarantee Act (NREGA) after the Father of the Nation, Mahatma Gandhi as Mahatma Gandhi National Rural Employment Guarantee Act (MNREGA) and observing 2009-10 as the *Year of the Gram Sabha* by the Prime Minister Dr. Manmohan Singh in the presence of the UPA Chairperson Sonia Gandhi, Panchayati Raj and Rural Development Minister, Dr. C.P. Joshi and a large number of gram pradhans, sarpanchs and village representatives from all over the country.

In his keynote address, the Prime Minister said that Panchayati Raj institutions need to play a pivotal role in the nation's development. Highlighting the fact that peoples' participation is a must to implement the government's programmes and schemes in a transparent and effective manner, he called upon Panchayati Raj institutions to take the lead. Dr. Singh stressed the need to strive continuously to make panchayati raj institutions effective instruments of people's power. On observing 2009-10 as the *Year of the Gram Sabha*, the Prime Minister said that the gram sabha provides a forum for villagers to discuss, deliberate, accept or reject the proposals of the gram panchayat. Dr. Singh said that the decision to rename the National Rural Employment Guarantee Act (NREGA) as the Mahatma Gandhi National Rural Employment Guarantee Act (MNREGA) was a humble tribute to the Father of our nation.

About major achievements and initiatives of the Ministry of Rural Development & Panchayati Raj see Annexure.

OBSERVATIONS ABOUT WAGES PAID UNDER THE NREGA SCHEME

Sonia Gandhi suggested a nationally-aligned minimum wage. UPA Chairperson Sonia Gandhi has written[5] to the Prime Minister Manmohan Singh, recommending that wages paid under the UPA's flagship rural employment guarantee scheme, be reconciled with the statutory minimum wages. If implemented, this will affect workers in 19 states, where the states' minimum wages exceed the centrally fixed Rs. 100 daily wage under the scheme.

In January 2009, the Centre froze wages to be paid under the Mahatma Gandhi National Rural Employment Guarantee Scheme (MGNREGS) at Rs. 100, as it was felt that some states tended to increase the minimum wage arbitrarily. The minimum wages of 19 states, including Rajasthan, Andhra Pradesh, Chhattisgarh, Jharkhand, Bihar, Karnataka and Kerala, are higher than Rs. 100. Consequently, workers under MGNREGS were being paid less than the statutory minimum wage. "This is a totally unacceptable situation and needs to be corrected at once," says the background note attached by Sonia to her letter to the PM, written on 11 November, 2010.

Indira Jaising noted Additional Solicitor General said "The payment of wages below the minimum wage would amount to forced labour."

Labour groups in Andhra Pradesh went to the High Court against the issue and the Ministry's notification stands suspended until further orders in Andhra Pradesh. The Chief Ministers of Andhra Pradesh and Rajasthan wrote to the PM requesting reconciliation of wages to the minimum wage levels.

The *Mazdoor Kisan Shakti Sangathan* led by the Magsaysay awardee, Aruna Roy had been sitting in *dharna* in Jaipur since October, 2010 on this issue. The matter was also raised by Roy, Economist Jean Dreze and 'Right to Food' campaigner, Harsh Mander in meetings of the National Advisory Council Chaired by Sonia. On October 23, members of the NAC reached a consensus on this issue, she wrote in her note to the PM.

The background note to the letter suggests that the practical solution of the situation would be for the centre to immediately notify the prevailing minimum wage rates in each state, as the rate to be paid under the MNREGA with a stipulation that the approved minimum wage would then be indexed to inflation, as measured by the consumer price index for agricultural labour.

As for future increases, beyond inflation adjustment, it suggests that the MNERGA rates be arrived at through a tripartite consultative process involving the centre, the state governments and representatives of workers. Such a process, it is suggested would protect the interests of the workers, while removing the fiscal uncertainty that characterizes a situation in which states can arbitrarily hike wage rates, while the centre has to foot the bill.

THREAT TO THE MINIMUM WAGE STRUCTURE

The Prime Minister's observations in the *Times of India*[6] of 6 January, 2011, reported that the consensual view that emerged after discussions with the ministries involved, was that while MNREGA wages should remain delinked from the Minimum Wages Act, the government will protect a real wage of Rs. 100 per day, by indexing the wage rate to the Consumer Price Index for agricultural labourers, from 1 January, 2011.The base will be reset every five years. A committee under the Chairmanship of the Chief Statistician, Pronab Sen is working on an index for fixing MNREGA wages in the future, the letter adds. Members of the Rajasthan based *Mazdoor Kisan Shakti Sangathan* whose pioneering efforts contributed to the passage of the Employment Guarantee Act termed the PM's decision as a violation of a Constitutional right. "This represents a threat to the minimum wage structure which is the only buffer that the vulnerable have against inflation and arbitrary changes," Nikhil Dey of the MKSS told TOI. Inflation indexing, which is part of the Minimum Wages Act, will not by itself raise the wages of all MNREGA workers to the minimum wage, he added.

In January 2009, the Centre froze wages to be paid under MNREGA at Rs. 100, as it was felt that some states tended to increase the minimum wage arbitrarily. High inflation led several states to revise their minimum wages and as a result, the minimum wages of 19 states including Rajasthan, Andhra Pradesh, Chhattisgarh, Jharkhand, Bihar, Karnataka and Kerala are higher than Rs. 100 as of now, but not payable to MNREGA workers.

Labour groups in Andhra Pradesh went to the High Court which expressed its displeasure and suspended the Ministry's notification in Andhra Pradesh. The MKSS led by the Magsaysay awardee Aruna Roy sat in *dharana* in Jaipur for 45 days over the issue. The matter was also raised by Roy, economist Jean Dreze and Right to Food campaigner Harsh Mander in meetings of the NAC chaired by Sonia, the details of which are given in the previous news item of TOI dated 13 November, 2010.

In view of this, the Prime Minister Manmohan Singh has shot down the Sonia Gandhi headed National Advisory Council's recommendation that the National Rural Employment Guarantee Scheme (NREGS) workers be paid minimum wages set by states. The Prime Minister, in his December 31 letter to the UPA Chairperson, clarified that the wage rate fixed by the Central Government would be indexed to inflation, but not linked to the Minimum Wages Act.

CHALLENGES

There are many challenges before PRIs. It is to be seen to what extent the PRIs can fulfill people's aspirations. A majority of which are:

1. Article 40 in Chapter IV of the Constitution envisages that the state shall take steps to organise village panchayats, and endow them with such powers and authority as may be necessary to enable them to function as units of self-

government. It is observed that the Directive Principles of State Policy do not have the force of law, and are not justifiable. Here there is need that village panchayats may function to the entire satisfaction of the people, and inspire and motivate them to elicit people's cooperation in development activities.

2. The people in general are showing increasing signs of restlessness and disenchantment with the political process, as there is a wide difference between promise and performance, and PRIs have been given a chance again to come upto the expectations of the people, to have a clear nexus between votes and the welfare of the citizens.

3. People in general are not much interested in what is happening around the world, but they do feel agitated and disturbed when their daily routine life is disturbed due to power breakdowns, non-supply of water, telephone lines out of order every now and then, no proper sanitation, no control over mosquitoes menace, non-availability of healthcare services, drainage and sewerage problems, no public conveyance for children to go to school, no street light and no one to repair roads which one has to traverse every day and night. It is thus the duty of the elected representatives to see to what extent they would be able to meet the daily demands of the people at the local level, through democratically elected bodies, so that there is sufficient time left to devote to other developmental work.

4. The democratic process loses all credibility when there is no accountability. For over 60 years, people have changed governments often through their votes and when even that fails, unrest, violence and disorder become the order of the day. It is high time to become cautious and be accountable to the people through their elected local bodies, to start in relatively small units of self-government. The situation has not changed even today.

5. The Chairman[7] of the Tenth Finance Commission has already cautioned the local governments in the states not to put their financial claims at a higher level. Much depended upon the recommendations of the Tenth Finance Commission made in pursuance of the new sub-clause (b) in clause (3) of Article 280 of the Constitution, inserted by the Seventy-third Constitutional Amendment. The new sub-clause 280(3) (bb), makes it obligatory on the National Finance Commission to make recommendations to the President as to "the measures needed to augment the Consolidated Fund of a state to supplement the resources of the Panchayats in the state on the basis of recommendations made by the Finance Commission of the state. In any case, the National Finance Commission would be free to make any other recommendations on this behalf for each state, depending upon the tax

resources assigned/appropriated and grants-in-aid given to the PRIs in the state by the state government. It is but natural that progressive states in this regard would, certainly receive fewer amounts on this account as a result of the recommendations of the National Finance Commission. State governments' role should be to broaden the tax base of the PRIs themselves, and to assign and appropriate lucrative state taxes to the PRIs.

6. After the passing of the 73rd & 74th Amendment, the Commission is required to give recommendations to the President regarding:

    (i) The distribution between the union and the states of the net proceeds of taxes which are to be, or may be divided between them, and the allocation between the states of the respective shares of such proceeds. The principles which should govern the grants in-aid of the revenues of the states out of the Consolidated Fund of India.

    (ii) The measures needed to augment the Consolidated Fund of a state to supplement the resources of the Panchayats in the state on the basis of the recommendations made by the Finance Commission of the state; The measures needed to augment the Consolidated Fund of a state to supplement the resources of the municipalities in the states, on the basis of the recommendations made by the Finance Commission of the states; any other matter referred to the Commission by the President in the interests of sound finance.

7. The Twelfth Finance Commission[8] had recommended that a sum of Rs. 20,000 crore be made available as grants to state governments during the period 2005-2010 to augment the Consolidated Fund at state levels, to facilitate supplementing of the financial resources placed at the disposal of the Panchayats

8. The Thirteenth Finance Commission[9] in its award for the period 2010-2015, has made comprehensive observations and recommendations regarding empowerment of the local bodies and devolution of funds to these bodies. While recommending grants for local bodies, 13th FC made a departure from its predecessors, which recommended a specific quantum of grant. The 13th FC instead has recommended grants as a percentage of the net proceeds of the union taxes of the previous year. Although the amount recommended is a percent of the divisible pool, it has been recommended that it should be converted into grant-in-aid under Article 275 of the Constitution while transferring to the local bodies. To ensure that the valuable of the grant is commensurable at the start of the year, it has been linked to the divisible pool of the previous year. The grants recommended by the 13th FC has two components: a basic component and a performance based component. The

basic grant is recommended to be equivalent to 1.5 per cent of the net proceeds of the union taxes of the previous year. The performance grant, effective from 2010-2011 is recommended to be 0.5 per cent of the net proceeds in 2011-12 and 1 per cent thereafter.

9. If so, the responsibility for utilising the tax sources to the maximum extent possible would devolve on the PRIs in the states. It would thus give the surest guarantee for the strength, as well as the autonomy of the PRIs. Leadership, will power, imagination and tactfulness of the PRIs would go a long way in strengthening the financial base of such PRIs. Periodical elections to PRIs, and frequent change in leadership for better functioning should be kept in view.

10. Mere representation of women in these bodies has not helped the women of every strata, Indira Gandhi once said, "if a handful of women go forward, become ministers or judges, you should not think that women's status has gone up." Justice Krishna Aiyer has also analysed what is meant by equality of men and women. He says that equality of men and women does not mean identity of individuality, and does not negate differences in personality. What is equal, is the acceptance that women shall be free to unfold her full potential in the social milieu in which she is cast.

11. Globally, women are making rapid strides in education and health, while lagging behind men in economic and political status. We have thus to watch and see to what extent the reservation for women in PRIs would bring participation of women at the political and economic levels, for the upliftment of this class of society.

PANCHAYATI RAJ AND THE GLOBAL SCENARIO

Developing and developed countries across the world are also showing immense interest in the successful functioning of the institutions of Panchayati Raj in India. India is also eager to learn, inter alia, from Asian, Commonwealth, and Western countries, where local governance is successfully addressing the felt and perceived needs of local committees. The following initiatives of the Ministry of Panchayati Raj cover three broad areas, i.e. bilateral cooperation, interaction with multilateral agencies, and linking up with the common fora dealing with local self government with other countries.[10]

Afghanistan

On 17 May 2008, the Ministry of Panchayati Raj (MoPR) signed an MoU on "Cooperation in the field of local governance" with the Minister, Rural Rehabilitation and Development,

Government of Afghanistan and in pursuance, the training programme on *Management of Rural Development and Good Governance* was held from 29 September to 19 October, 2009 in which 25 Afghan officials participated at NIRD, Hyderabad.

A three weeks international training programme was organized by NIRD, Hyderabad for the Afghanistan officials. The participants included UNDP officials, District Governors, Secretaries, Directors, Social activists and other government officials. The programme content included concepts namely, decentralised governance, good governance, poverty indicators, agriculture scenario strategies, rural development strategies, rural developmental programmes, national rural employment guarantee programme, housing, drinking water and sanitation, rural connectivity, rural infrastructure, self help groups, public distribution system in villages, health bodies, social audit, right to information, developmental efforts taken up in Afghanistan, district representatives and villagers were organized in four gram panchayats, district collectors and Zila Parishad presidents and other senior level officials interacted with them in their respective districts. Ten days field visits to six districts within Andhra Pradesh, and three days in Mysore was also organized to show the ground realities in the functioning of the programmes.

Norway

In order to strengthen local democracy between India and Norway, a draft MoU was approved in February 2009 by the Government of India. The objective is to encourage transference of competence between the two countries for strengthening local self-governance, including capacity building of institutions, operationalising the mechanisms of Indo-Norway Joint Forum/Joint Working Group for bilateral exchange of elected representatives, civil society organizations, as well as intellectuals, researchers, resource persons and officials on both sides for future partnerships.

South Africa

On 12 August, 2008, a nine-member delegation led by Ms. Geraldine Fraser Moleketi, Minister of Public Service and Administration of the Republic of South Africa met the Minister and other officers of the Ministry of PR who were briefed about the Panchayati Raj system in India, from the ancient period to the present time, and made a presentation on the 73rd Amendment Act and about the schemes being operated by the Ministry. The Minister of Local Governance, South Africa recalled with a deep sense of appreciation the training programmes organized for the African officials in the NIRD (National Institute of Rural Development), Hyderabad. MoU in the field of governance, administration and other related areas are in progress.

Switzerland

Dr. Bernard Dafflon, Professor of Public Finance and Public Management, University of Fribourg, Switzerland during his visit to India in January 2009 on a mission for "Switzerland Knowledge Exchange Programme on Strengthening Fiscal Decentralisation," attended the National Conference of the Chairpersons and Chief Executive Officers of District Planning Commitees and Secretaries of State Planning and Panchayati Raj Departments, organized by the MoPR, and participated in an interactive meeting with Chairpersons/Secretaries of the State Finance Commission, State Secretaries of Finance and Panchayati Raj Departments, and other stakeholders. The MoPR and the Government of Switzerland (Swiss Confederation), Ministry of Foreign Affairs are contemplating signing an MoU for mutual cooperation in the area of local governance for mutual benefit of both the countries. A Foreign Office Consultation (FDC) between two countries was held on 5 December, 2009 where the entire gamut of bilateral relations was reviewed. The MoU is under consideration.

Commonwealth Local Government Forum (CLGF)

The Commonwealth Local Government Forum, which has presence in 39 countries of the Commonwealth with 150 members organizations, is a non-governmental forum established in 1995 with the objective to undertake activities, exchange information between countries on matters relating to local government.

The MoPR enrolled itself as a member of the Commonwealth Local Government Forum in March 2007, which would facilitate global interaction and exchange of ideas in respect of local governance, MoRP has continued its membership for the period April 2009–March 2010.

World Bank

The World Bank intends to provide financial and technical support to states for strengthening Panchayati Raj. Karnataka is the first state to have obtained funds under the World Bank aided Panchayat Strengthening Project, which has an outlay of US$ 120 million, to be spent in the form of untied fund allocations and capacity building for Panchayats in the state's poorest 39 taluks. The project started on 14 October, 2006 and will be completed on 31 March. 2012. Similar programmes are envisaged for Bihar, Kerala, and West Bengal. In 2009-2010, under the Chairmanship of Shri A.N.P. Sinha, Secretary, MoPR (SPR) with representatives of the World Bank and the state governments of Karnataka, West Bengal, Bihar and Kerala to discuss the World Bank assisted projects.

Study Tour to Switzerland and the United Kingdom

An Indian delegation consisting of 18 members including secretaries and senior level officers of the Governments of West Bengal, Karnataka, Assam, Madhya Pradesh, Andhra Pradesh, Gujarat, Rajasthan, Bihar, Orissa, Jharkhand, Maharashtra, Chhattisgarh and, the Ministry of Rural Development led by Shri Sudhir Krishna, Additional Secretary and Smt. Rashmi Shukla Sharma, Joint Secretary visited the United Kingdom and Switzerland from 16-25 February, 2010 to gain international exposure for strengthening local governance in India. The delegation studied in detail local government systems in these countries, and the states will incorporate the learnings thereof.

REFERENCES

[1] From a part of H.R. Bangia's article on "Panchayati Raj & Seventy Third Constitutional Amendment" *Dreams and Realities – Expectations from Panchayati Raj*, Indian Institute of Public Administration, New Delhi (1996) pp - 55-62.

[2] Report: Ministry of Panchayati Raj, Government of India's Annual Report 2009-10.

[3] Ibid.

[4] Ibid.

[5] The Times of India dated 13 November, 2010.

[6] *The Times of India* dated 6 January, 2011.

[7] Ibid.

[8] Ibid.

[9] Ibid.

[10] Ibid.

ANNEXURE I

1. Agriculture and extension:
2. Land improvement land reforms, consolidation, soil and water conservation.
3. Minor irrigation, water management and watershed development.
4. Animal husbandry, dairying, poultry, etc.
5. Fisheries.
6. Social and farm forestry.
7. Fuel and fodder.
8. Minor forest products.
9. Non-conventional energy sources.
10. Small industries including food processing.
11. Khadi Village and Cottage Industries.
12. Roads, culverts, bridges, ferries, waterways and other means of communication.
13. Rural electrification including distribution of electricity.
14. Drinking water.
15. Rural housing.
16. Education including primary and secondary schools.
17. Technical and vocational education.
18. Adult and non-formal education.
19. Libraries.
20. Cultural activities, festivals, etc.
21. Health, sanitation including hospitals and dispensaries.
22. Family welfare.
23. Public distribution system.
24. Markets and fairs.
25. Women and child welfare.
26. Social welfare including welfare of handicapped and mentally retarded.
27. Social welfare of scheduled castes and scheduled tribes.
28. Poverty alleviation programmes.
29. Maintenance of community assets.

ANNEXURE II

MAJOR ACHIEVEMENTS AND INITIATIVES OF THE MINISTRY OF RURAL DEVELOPMENT & PANCHAYATI RAJ, GOVERNMENT OF INDIA

1. **National Conference of Chairpersons/CEOs of District Planning Committees.** A two-day National Conference of Chairpersons/CEOs of District Planning Committees was inaugurated by the Prime Minister Dr. Manmohan Singh in New Delhi on 16 January, 2009. Speaking on the occasion Dr. Singh said, "Every plan must start with a vision and it is important for us to look at what our collective vision ought to be. To my mind, the most important issues before us are to meet the challenge of reducing inequity and inequality.

   Following the envisioning process, a plan will need to emerge from the Gram Sabha at the village level upwards". This is also an appropriate time to fit together priorities that cut across the jurisdictions of Gram Panchayats and municipalities into larger projects. Finally, it is for the District Planning Committees to consolidate the urban and rural plans into draft development plans for the district as a whole. The next step is to match resources with the plan.

2. **Centrally Sponsored Schemes.** Over the past nearly five years, central government transfers to Centrally Sponsored Schemes (CSS) have increased nearly threefold from Rs. 36,000 crores in 2004-05 to Rs. 1,20,000 crores in 2008-09. The top 15 CSS with the NREGA at the forefront, now account for nearly Rs. 85,000 crores. Of all the provisions in the 73rd and 74th Amendments, Article 243 ZD of the Constitution which provides for District Planning Committees has perhaps been the last to be implemented in full measure. Till four years back, only 12 of the 24 states to which the Panchayati Raj and Nagarpalika provisions of the Constitution applied, had constituted DPCs.

3. **National Conference of the Chairpersons of the District Planning Committees.** The Ministry of Panchayati Raj along with the Planning Commission and the Ministry of Urban Development organized a National Conference of the Chairpersons of the District Planning Committees. The Chairpersons of the Zilla Parishads, Chief Executive Officers of the Zilla Parishads, representatives of the national institutions involved in supporting the process of district planning and state institutes of rural development participated in the conference.

4. **National Consultation – Academics for Panchayati Raj.** A 2-day National Consultation – Academics for Panchayati Raj began in New Delhi on 25 February, 2009. The National Consultation with luminaries from the field of academics was

inaugurated by Shri Mani Shankar Aiyar, the Minister of Panchayati Raj and Development of the North East Region, to deliberate on the important issues relating to effective implementation of Panchayati Raj in the country. Shri Aiyar said on the occasion that academics whose voices matter, have assembled for the first time to ponder over the subject of Panchayati Raj and its implementation. These deliberations at higher intellectual levels would surely provide a completely fresh boost to the Local Governments (LGs), the Minister added. On the occasion, the Minister also released a book titled "Panchayati Raj and Local Governance: Through the Eyes of Writers and Thinkers".

5. **Seminar on Findings of Nationwide Survey on Elected Women Representatives in Panchayats.** Shri Mani Shankar Aiyer, the then Minister of Panchayati Raj and Development of the North Eastern region has said that with 12 lakh Elected Women Representatives (EWRs) of *panchayats*, the public image of women has changed drastically in India. Women have been empowered politically and socially, and the level of social and political empowerment is without a parallel anywhere in the world. Shri Aiyer said this, while inaugurating a two-day National Seminar on *Findings of the Study on Elected Women Representatives in Village Panchayats* here on 2 March, 2009. The objective of the seminar was to promote a dialogue between the intellectual and experts engaged in the field of Panchayati Raj, and its working and the women representatives of panchayats functioning at the grassroots level.

6. **Panchayat Empowerment & Accountability Incentive Scheme (PEAIS) – Assessment of the States.** The Panchayat Empowerment & Accountability Incentive Scheme (PEAIS) has been introduced in, and implemented by the Ministry of Panchayati Raj (MoPR) since 2005-06. The scheme aims at encouraging the states for adequately empowering the Panchayati Raj Institutions (PRIs), and putting in place arrangements for bringing about accountability of the PRIs. Performance of the states is measured through a Devolution Index (DI). A token award is also given to the states, for which the annual provision is currently at Rs. 10 crore.

For the year 2008-09, the Ministry decided to award 10 prizes in all, as follows:

First Prize (Top 4 States): Madhya Pradesh, West Bengal, Tamil Nadu, and Kerala Rs. 1.50 crore each.

Second Prize (Next 4 States): Karnataka, Sikkim, Himachal Pradesh, and Haryana. Rs. 75 lakh each.

Third Prize (Next 2 States): Chhattisgarh and Assam Rs. 50 lakh each.

7. **Seminar to discuss the findings of the "Study on Elected Women Representative in Village Panchayats."** A seminar was organized in partnership with the Department of Women Studies & Development Centre, Delhi University headed by Prof. Vibha

Chaturvedi, on 2-3 March, 2009 at Vigyan Bhawan, New Delhi, to discuss the findings of the study report. The seminar attended by over 150 persons, included well-known academics and researchers, representatives of state governments and training institutions. Around 50 elected women representatives also participated in the seminar. The deliberations of the seminar covered two days, when the conclusions of the study report, situation of Panchayati Raj and elected women representatives in the states and general issues relating to devolution of 3Fs, capacity building, etc., were discussed in great detail.

8. **Dr. C.P. Joshi.** Union Rural Development & Panchayati Raj Minister, Dr. C.P. Joshi stated on 03, July 2009 that consultative mechanisms have been set up to review the functioning of Panchayati Raj institutions (PRIs) in the states/UTs. These mechanisms at different levels, have been constantly monitoring the progress and implementation of decisions related to the devolution of powers to the Panchayati Raj Institutions. The Council of Ministers of Panchayati Raj chaired by the Minister of Panchayati Raj and Rural Development, reviewed the progress during the last three years in its meetings in August, 2007 and April 2008. In addition, a Committee of Chief Secretaries of states and Panchayati Raj Secretaries of the state governments chaired by the Union Secretary of Panchayati Raj has been set up to monitor the progress and implementation of the action points resulting from the round tables held previously. Six meetings of this committee were held during last three years. Various issues impinging on the functioning of PRIs were discussed by the Council of Ministers, and the Committee chaired by the Union Secretary of Panchayati Raj.

The issues include devolution of powers to PRIs, activity mapping, capacity building and training, setting up of District Planning Committee (DPCs) and preparation of district plan, IT enabled e-governance, role of gram sabhas, implementation of PESA, annual reports on the state of panchayats, centrality of PRIs in implementation of centrally sponsored schemes, rural business hubs through public-private-panchayat partnerships, accounting and audit, etc. state governments take necessary follow-up action on the decisions/action points emerging from these meeting.

9. **National Level Consultations with Panchayats.** The Ministry of Panchayati Raj and the Ministry of Agriculture have written to all concerned ministries and departments, agricultural universities and state governments to operationalise the national policy for farmers in accordance with the decisions taken /recommendations made during the National Consultation of Panchayats held last year on 16-17, March 2008. The Indian Council of Agriculture Research has also been requested to organise a conference of Vice-Chancellors of all the universities and other related organisations and PRIs in order to achieve greater technical support to farmers, by involving agriclutural universities students to strengthen the extension services at the grassroots level.

10. **Training the Panchayat and Gram Sabha Representatives – Computerisation of Panchayats.** The Minister for Panchayati Raj, Dr. C.P. Joshi informed the Lok Sabha on 10 July, 2009 that the Ministry is in the process of finalizing the scheme for e-governance in Panchayati Raj institutions. In reply to a written question in the Lok Sabha, he stated that in view of the strategic importance of computerisation at the gram panchayat level, the Ministry of Panchayati Raj (MoPR) had constituted an expert group in June 2007 to assess the current and future Information Technology (IT) programmes of the ministry, to recommend on the most cost-effective technologies for reaching IT to the gram panchayats, the use of IT for effectively building capacities of Panchayati Raj institutions through distance learning; and the cost implications of the recommendations.

11. **Programs and Schemes for Panchayati Raj.** Efforts have been made by the Union Ministry of Panchayati Raj to supplement the work undertaken by the State Governments to empower the panchayats through a series of schemes. These schemes include :

    Panchayat Empowerment & Accountability Incentive Scheme (PEIAS);

    Rashtriya Gram Swaraj Yojana;

    Panchayat Mahila & Yuva Shakti Abhiyan;

    Backward Regions Grant Fund and Rural Business Hubs.

    Under the Panchayat Empowerment & Accountability Incentive Scheme (PEIAS) the state governments are encouraged to empower the Panchayati Raj Institutions (PRIs) by providing incentives for the devolution of functions, funds and functionaries to the PRIs, and prizes are given to better performing states. During the year 2008-09, Madhya Pradesh, West Bengal, Tamil Nadu, Kerala, Karnataka, Sikkim, Himachal Pradesh, Haryana, Chhattisgarh and Assam got prizes.

12. **Every Panchayat to have a Bharat Nirman Rajiv Gandhi Sewa Kendra and Panchayat Ghar over the next three years:** *Dr. C.P. Joshi.* All the Gram Panchayats across the country will have a panchayat ghar and a Bharat Nirman Rajiv Gandhi Sewa Kendra over the next three years. This was announced by the Union Panchayati Raj Minister Dr. C.P. Joshi at a National Workshop on NREGA , *NREGA: A Step Towards Governance Reform, Transparency and Accountability* in Vigyan Bhawan organized by the Union Ministry Of Rural Development on the occasion of the birth anniversary of former Prime Minister Rajiv Gandhi on 20 August, 2009. There are 2.52 lakh gram panchayats across the country. The proposed panchayat ghars have been envisaged as a mini secretariat and as a forum for the rural people to meet, share and discuss their issues, to provide logistic support and as a record keeping facility center.

The Bharat Nirman Rajiv Gandhi Sewa Kendra is a single window for providing information on the NREGS and shall provide feedback on the quality of implementation of the program. The idea is to slowly move on wage employment to self employment, by providing skill development facilities to the rural people, and in the process give a fillip to the rural economy. The proposed design of the Bharat Nirman Sewa Kendra at every gram panchayat was unveiled on this occasion by Shri Rahul Gandhi, the guest of honour of the workshop.

13. **Dr. C.P. Joshi highlighted quarterly achievements of the Panchayati Raj Ministry** Union Minister for Rural Development and Panchayati Raj, Dr. C.P. Joshi on 15 September, 2009 rolled out the quarterly progress report for the Ministry of Panchayati Raj on the occasion of the completion of 100 days of the present UPA government. Addressing media persons here, the Minister said at present the Ministry of Panchayati Raj is concerned with the Amendment to Article 243D of the Constitution, for enhancing reservation for women in panchayats to 50 per cent along with the Restructuring of Backward Region Grant Fund (BRGF).

Quoting the Presidential address of 04 June, 2009 in Parliament, Dr. Joshi said in tune with the intention of the President of India to provide fifty percent reservations for women in panchayats by Amending *Article 243D of the Constitution*, as women suffer multiple deprivations of class, caste and gender, and enhancing reservation in panchayats, the Cabinet on 27 August, 2009 approved the proposal for moving a Constitutional Amendment Bill for enhancing reservation for women in panchayats at all tiers from one third at least to 50 per cent in the total number of seats. The proposed amendment will increase reservation for women in (i) the total number of seats to be filled by direct election, (ii) offices of chairpersons, and (iii) in seats and offices of chairpersons reserved for SCs and STs, to 50 percent in all tiers of panchayats. The Ministry of Panchayati Raj will move a Bill for amendment to Article 243D of the Constitution at the earliest. He said this step will lead to more women entering public sphere.

He said, according to Article 243G of the Constitution, state legislatures may endow panchayats with such powers and authority as may be necessary (i) to enable them to function as units of local self-government (LSG), and (ii) to prepare and implement plans/or schemes for economic development and social justice, including those in relation to matters listed in the Eleventh Schedule of the Constitution.

14. **2009 – 10 was the year of Gram Sabha** Panchayati Raj in India completed 50 years on 2 October, 2009. To commemorate the occasion, a National Convention of Panchayati Raj Ministers, Zila Parishad Presidents and elected representatives who have served more than 25 years from all the States/UTs was organized by the Ministry

of Panchayati Raj at Vigyan Bhawan. A function at Nagaur in Rajasthan was also organized later in the evening on this occasion.

It may be recalled that the Late Pt. Jawaharlal Nehru, the first Prime Minister of India, had inaugurated Panchayati Raj in India at Naguar in Rajasthan on 2 October, 1959.

15. **NREGA renamed after Mahatma Gandhi as MGNREGA on 2 October, 2009.**

16. **28 Panchayats Honoured for Making Their Villages 'Open-defecation Free' and Nirmal Villages.** "Good sanitation practices are the key to a healthy life style" and the total sanitation campaign has generated a lot of enthusiasm among the rural people, making it truly a people's campaign. This was the message from the President, Smt. Pratibha Devisingh Patil, while presenting the Nirmal Gram Puraskars for the year 2009 at a function held in Vigyan Bhawan, New Delhi. Smt. Patil said it is essential that the presidents of gram panchayats play a pivotal role in sanitation promotion, as they reflect the will of the people at grassroots level. She called on all the winning panchayats to sustain the level of sanitation they have achieved. Over 1000 awardees and invitees gathered for Nirmal Gram Puraskar function, where 28 block panchayats and two district panchayats attained the Nirmal status of being open defecation free, received the award from the President.

17. **Participatory Planning and convergence of schemes & resources by Panchayati Raj Institutions important for implementation of Rural Development Schemes –** *Dr. C.P. Joshi,* Union Rural Development and Panchayati Raj Minister emphasized the criticality of participatory planning and convergence of schemes and resources, in implementing different rural development schemes. In a letter written to all Chief Ministers of respective states, he has urged them to chalk out their strategies in view of the exigencies of a drought like situation in large parts of the country. The minister says that this has made it imperative to strengthen PRIs, as it calls for massive planning of works not only under NREGA, but also under other relevant schemes (viz. Integrated Watershed Management Programme, Minor Irrigation, SGSY, Drinking Water, etc.), and greatly improved implementation in saving the planted crops, providing livelihood and conserving soil and water for the future.

The Minister recalled that panchayats at the district, intermediate and village levels, are the principal authorities for planning and implementation of NREGA under Section 13 of the Act. Also, the main responsibilities of PRIs are outlined in Sections 13 to 17. Moreover, at least 50 percent of NREGA funds are to be spent directly by the Gram Panchayats (GPs). Gram Sabhas (GSs) are to recommend specific projects to GPs, and conduct social audit of NREGA works. Dr. Joshi said these features of NREGA offer on unique opportunity to strengthen and enable PRIs, particularly the GPs and GSs.

18. **Revamping of Panchayati Raj Institutions.** The Minister of Panchayati Raj, Dr. C.P. Joshi on 23 November, 2009 informed the Lok Sabha in reply to a written question on revamping of panchayati raj institutions, that the recommendations of the Sarkaria Commission on centre-state relations relating to PRIs, pertain to decentralization in planning.

The 73rd and 74th Constitution Amendments have mandated the establishment of the District Planning Committee (DPC) for consolidating plans prepared by panchayats and municipalities in districts into the draft District Plan. The Eleventh Plan, which has identified inclusive growth as its core vision, seeks to 'substantially empower and use PRIs as the primary means of delivery of essential services that are critical for inclusive growth.' The Plan asserts that 'it is absolutely critical for the inclusiveness of our growth process that has large numbers of elected representatives of PRIs are fully involved in planning, implementing and supervising the delivery of essential public services.' A detailed road map as to how this could be achieved, has been elaborated in the plan document in Chapter 10 entitled *Governance*, which recognizes decentralization and strengthening of PRIs as a major challenge.

Of the 24 states where Parts IX and IXA of the Constitution are applicable, District Planning Committees have been constituted in 22 states, i.e. in all states except Jharkhand and Uttarakhand. The Planning Commission has also released a Manual for Integrated District Planning, which the states can use as a handbook for participatory grassroots level planning. Also, there is no proposal to appoint any commission to revamp the Panchayati Raj institutions.

19. **Meeting of Principal Secretaries (Panchayati Raj) Held.** Dr. C.P. Joshi, Union Minister of Panchayati Raj & Rural Development, addressed the Principal Secretaries (PR) from all the states at the Vigyan Bhawan on 27 November, 2009.. He advised them to take personal interest in promoting the cause of panchayats so that the system all over the country is comparable, or even better than that of the best performing states. The immediate areas where panchayats should focus are those related to the Human Development Index, and activities covering elementary education, health and sanitation, integrated child development, women development, etc. In a day-long meeting held at Vigyan Bhawan, Shri A.N.P. Sinha, Union Secretary, Panchayati Raj reviewed the action taken by the state governments in observing 2009-10 as the "Year of Gram Sabha", embedding panchayats in NREGA and other proposals, preparation of integrated plans at the gram panchayat level, capacity building of panchayats and the progress of backward regions grant fund, the flagship programme implemented through the Ministry of Panchayati Raj.

Is Finance Accessible to All in South Asia?

Rashmi Umesh Arora

Department of Accounting, Finance and Economics
Griffith Business School, Griffith University

ABSTRACT

Financial access is gradually being recognised as an important input for economic development. This study using World Bank (2007) and CGAP (2009) database, examines the extent of financial access in South Asian countries. The results of the study show that India ranks highest among all the South Asian countries.

Keywords: Financial Access, India, South Asia, Development

JEL Classification: O16, O53, G21

INTRODUCTION

Access to finance can be defined as "availability of a supply of reasonable quality financial services at reasonable costs, where reasonable quality and reasonable cost have to be defined relative to some objective standard, with costs reflecting all pecuniary and non-pecuniary costs" (Claessens 2006). It can also be defined as the "absence of price and non-price barriers" (Demirguc-Kunt and Levine 2008). Access could include access to various financial products and services, bank accounts, bank credit, savings products, remittances and payment services, insurance services, home mortgage and financial advisory services.

Financial access eases the external financing constraint that prevents firms' expansion. Poor access to finance also leads to increased income inequalities, poverty, and low growth rates. Thus, access to finance and inclusive financial system which includes all groups of people, has been advocated to reduce inequalities and poverty in developing countries[1] (World Bank 2008; Claessens and Feijen 2007). Beck, Demirguc-Kunt et al. (2009) observed that, "without inclusive financial systems, poor individuals and small enterprises need to rely on their personal wealth or internal resources to invest in their education, become entrepreneurs, or take advantage of promising growth opportunities." In India "broad approach to financial inclusion aims at 'connecting people' with the banking system and not just credit dispensation; giving people access to payments system and portray financial inclusion as a viable business model and opportunity" (RBI 2008).

Ambiguity, however, surrounds appropriate measures of financial access. Availability of credit is often considered as the closest indicator of the level of financial services accessible to people in different countries. Credit, however, cannot be the sole indicator, as the financial intermediaries perform several other functions, besides providing credit such as they accelerate the savings rate by offering savings products of different maturities and yields, and allocate these resources to increase investment. They also reduce risks across projects, firms, and industries by risk diversification, through which they accelerate technological change and economic growth. By opening bank branches far and wide, banks also develop banking habits (practice of going to the banks, and performing banking transactions) among the population in the early stages of economic development (Porter 1966), the In less developed countries where property rights are not well developed, the large informal sector is present, financial systems are not well developed and requirements of collateral exist, credit is not very often the most sought after financial product by the people. In these situations, banks are very often used as the safe custodian and holders of deposits and large sections of the poor population performs simple functions of withdrawing and depositing funds of small denominations. Our study, therefore, instead of taking credit as the sole indicator, adopts a multiple indicator and multi-dimensional approach, and using World Bank database covers as many dimensions of financial access as possible.

Our objective in this study is to examine financial access of countries within the South Asia region (Afghanistan, Bangladesh, Bhutan, Maldives, Nepal, Pakistan, Sri Lanka, and India). Due to data limitations, the study excludes Bhutan, Afghanistan and Maldives from the analysis, and is restricted to major countries in the region- Bangladesh, Nepal, Pakistan, Sri Lanka, and India. This region was chosen as it is fast growing, yet has high levels of poverty and low human capital development. Further, huge demand for finance in

---

[1] It, however, remains unclear what is the impact of the financial sector on income distribution, and whether it is more important to promote efficiency in the financial sector or expand access or both.

South Asia and its lack of accessibility has been noted by other studies. Fernando (2007) emphasised that:

"Closing the huge gap between the demand for financial services from low-income households and its supply from the formal and semiformal sources in both quantitative and qualitative terms may be considered one of the biggest development challenges facing most developing countries in Asia and other regions."

Our study builds two sets of financial access indices, covering banks and non-banks including microfinance separately. The results of our study show that financial access (FAI-I) is highest in India among all the South Asian countries, followed by Sri Lanka, Bangladesh, Pakistan, and Nepal. Sri Lanka, on the other hand, topped among all the South Asian countries followed by India in access to finance provided by non-banking institutions, including microfinance. Our study contributes to the literature on finance in South Asia, and to the literature on financial access in general. Few empirical studies exist in the area of financial access, perhaps due to lack of data on many access variables at the country level. This study by using recently available World Bank (2007) and also CGAP (2009) databases, attempts to build financial access index for South Asian countries.

The rest of the article is organised as follows. Section 2 provides a brief sketch of the economic growth in the region, and highlights low capital accumulation in the region. Section 3 spells out data and methodology on developing financial inclusion index in the South Asia region. Section 4 shows the results of the study. Section 5 concludes.

ECONOMIES OF THE SOUTH ASIA REGION

In terms of population size, South Asia comprises countries, both large and small. While India is a large country with a population of 1.2 billion and has 74 per cent of the region's population, at the other end is Maldives a small country with a population of 300,000. Table 1 shows the real average economic growth rate of the countries. Excluding conflict prone country Afghanistan, the average real growth rate in the region was 5.3 per cent during the period 1991-2000 and higher at 6.8 per cent during 2001-09.

The growth picked up from 2003 onwards, mainly due to high growth rates of India, Sri Lanka, and Pakistan. Although the countries have achieved high economic growth rates in recent years, yet it still remains far below what was achieved by the countries in the East Asia region. The major challenges which constrain growth are presence of high income inequality; persistence of conflict, corruption and high fiscal deficit. Also, South Asia lags behind East Asia, not only in terms of export orientation; inflow of foreign direct investment; skill levels; infrastructure and ease of doing business, but also in respect of savings[2], investment and productivity (Devarajan and Nabi 2006; Collins 2007).

Table 1: Average Annual Growth Rate of South Asian Countries

Countries	Average 1991-2000	2001	2002	2003	2004	2005	2006	2007	2008	2009	Average 2001-2009
Afghanistan	-	-	-	15.1	8.8	16.1	8.2	12.1	3.4	9.0	10.4
Bangladesh	4.9	4.8	4.8	5.8	6.1	6.3	6.5	6.3	5.6	5.0	5.7
Bhutan	5.0	6.8	10.9	7.2	6.8	7.0	8.8	17.9	6.6	5.7	8.6
Maldives	7.5	3.5	6.5	8.5	9.5	-4.6	18.0	7.2	5.7	-1.3	8.4
Nepal	5.0	5.6	0.1	3.9	4.7	3.1	3.7	3.2	4.7	3.6	3.6
Pakistan	3.9	2.0	3.2	4.8	7.4	7.7	6.2	6.0	6.0	2.5	5.1
Sri Lanka	5.2	-1.5	4.0	5.9	5.4	6.2	7.7	6.8	6.0	2.2	5.5
India	5.6	3.9	4.6	6.9	7.9	9.2	9.8	9.3	7.3	5.4*	7.1
Average	5.3	3.6	4.9	7.3	7.1	6.4	8.6	8.6	5.7	4.0	6.8

Note: * According to the latest World Economic Outlook Update (IMF 2009), the growth rate for India has been revised to 5.4 per cent. Details for other countries are not available and data, therefore relate to latest data available in WEO, April 2009.

Source: World Bank online, World Economic Outlook, April 2009, IMF.

Although, the region more known for its high poverty rates, is now known for its high growth rates as shown earlier, with a focus on inclusiveness (Ghani and Ahmed 2009), yet poverty still continues to be high in the region. Table 2 shows the Human Poverty Index (HPI) in South Asia. HPI introduced first by UNDP in 1997, takes into account non-income indicators of deprivation: probability at birth of not surviving to age 40; adult illiteracy rate; and decent standard of living – a composite indicator comprised of percentage

---

[2] Gross domestic savings as percentage of GDP in India was 23.0 per cent during the period 1990-91 to 1991-2000. This rose to 30.3 per cent in 2000-01 to 2008-09. With improved performance of the private corporate sector and enhanced contribution of the public sector, gross domestic saving as per cent of GDP at current market prices was 37.7 per cent in 2008-09.

of population without drinking water, and percentage of children underweight for their age. Table 2 shows that the countries in the region rank far below in HPI. The income indictors of poverty reflected in population less than US $1.25 a day, show that almost 50 per cent and even more of the population falls below this level except Sri Lanka and Pakistan.

Table 2: Poverty in South Asia

Countries	Human Poverty Index (HPI)		Population below Income Poverty Line		National Poverty Line (2000-06)
	Rank	Value (%)	$1.25 a day (2000-07)	$2 a day (2000-07)	
Maldives	66	16.5	-	-	-
Sri Lanka	67	16.8	14.0	39.7	22.7
Bhutan	102	33.7	49.5	-	-
India	88	28.0	41.6	75.6	28.6
Pakistan	101	33.4	22.6	60.3	32.6
Nepal	99	32.1	55.1	77.6	30.9
Bangladesh	112	36.1	49.6	81.3	40.0
Afghanistan	135	59.8	-	-	-

Source: UNDP (2009).

Investment in the region as percentage of GDP was, on an average, 32 per cent of GDP during the period 2004-08. This varied from 20.5 per cent in Pakistan to 50.5 per cent in Bhutan (Figure 1).

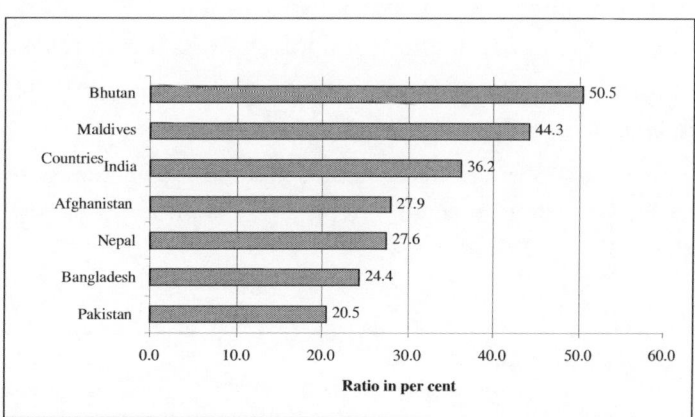

Fig. 1. Gross Capital Formation as % of GDP

DATA AND METHODOLOGY

Considering the immense significance of access to finance, and the need for financial inclusion for all and the region's high poverty level, in this study we develop a financial access index and suggest that economic development of the country should be judged by the level of country's financially inclusive development.

Dimensions of Access to Finance

Different dimensions of access to finance could be easy physical access, flexibility, and reliability (Beck, Demirgüç-Kunt and Honohan 2009; Fernando 2007; Sophastienphong and Kulathunga 2008).[3] Sophastienphong and Kulathunga (2008) in their study on South Asian financial development, take six indicators of banking access into account. These are demographic bank and ATM penetration (branches/ATM per 100,000 population); deposit and loan account per 1000 people; branches/ATM per 1000 square km (geographic branches/ATM per 1000 sq. km). The three dimensions of an inclusive financial system in Sarma (2008) were banking penetration (number of bank accounts as proportion of total population); availability of banking services (number of bank branches per 1000 population); usage dimension (bank credit and bank deposit as percentage of GDP).

Ideally one should take into consideration all the dimensions for arriving at a comprehensive picture on the inclusive financial system across the countries. However, data availability constraints prevent us from achieving this objective. Nevertheless, to cover the inclusiveness of the financial system in its various possible dimensions in a three pillared approach, we consider: how many people does it cover- geographically and demographically (physical access or outreach dimension); how easy is it to undertake transactions (ease dimension); and how much does it cost (cost dimension). Our choice of different dimensions is an improvement over Sarma (2008) in two respects:

(i) The multiple indicator approach in our study is in contrast to single indicator in each dimension as in Sarma (2008);

(ii) Sarma (2008) also does not take into account the time taken (ease of transactions) and transaction costs into account. Our study is an improvement in this respect.

---

[3] De La Torre, A., J.C. Gozzi, et al. (2007). "Financial Development: Maturing and Emerging Policy Issues." The World Bank Research Observer 22(1): 67-102 expressing concern on the emerging policy issues yet to be tackled by the policy makers, regarding financial sector development noted lack of finance to the small scale firms, stock market development; and pension system. Yet they did not discuss the issues relating to access to finance.

Table 3 provides a list of all the variables considered in our study

Table 3: Variables Used in the Study

Outreach	Ease	Cost
Geographic branch penetration (number of branches per 1000 sq km)	Locations to open deposit account	Fees consumer loan (% of minimum loan amount)
Demographic branch penetration (number of branches per 100,000 people)	Minimum amount to open checking account	Fees mortgage loan (% of minimum loan amount)
Geographic ATM penetration (number of ATMs per 1000 sq km)	Minimum amount to open savings account	Annual fees checking account
Demographic ATM penetration (number of ATMs per 100,000 people)	Minimum amount to be maintained in checking account	Annual fees savings account
	Minimum amount to be maintained in savings account	Cost to transfer funds internationally (% of US $250)
	Number of documents to open checking account	Amount of fees for using ATM cards (% of US $100)
	Number of documents to open savings account	
	Locations to submit loan applications	
	Minimum amount of consumer loan	
	Minimum amount of mortgage loan	
	Days to process consumer loan application	
	Days to process mortgage loan application	

Physical Access or Outreach (Dimension I)

Physical access, that is, presence of bank branches is often considered the most important source of access to finance in developing countries. Despite the notion of branchless banking and availability of ATM machines, yet easy access to a normal bank branch staffed with people, is still very important in the less developed areas. Also easy access to bank branches, as Porter (1966) pointed out, develops the habit of banking which leads to increased savings and investments, improve the efficiency of allocation of capital, and increase the ability of monetary authorities to stabilise the economy. Lewis (1955) also argued:

Experience shows that the amount of savings depends partly on how widespread these facilities (i.e. savings institutions) are: if they are pushed right under the individual's nose—people save more than if the nearest saving institution is some distance away.

In our study too, outreach (comprising four variables), both in geographic and demographic terms, constitutes an important dimension of access to finance.

Ease of Transactions (Dimension II)

The other two dimensions considered in our study are ease of transactions (12 variables considered) and cost of transactions (6 variables). On locations to open deposit accounts, the World Bank database assigns the value of 1, if an account can be opened at headquarters only; 2 if at headquarters or branch; and 3 if at headquarters, branches or a non-bank outlet. Minimum amount to open (to be maintained in) a checking or savings account is the minimum balance to open (maintain) a checking (savings) account. The number of documents needed to open a bank account range from 1 to 5, and could be documents for identification, payment slip, letter of reference, proof of domicile and other documents. As in the case of locations to open deposit accounts, as per the World Bank database, the locations to submit loan applications take the value 1, if applications can be submitted at headquarters only; 2 if at headquarters or branch; 3 if at headquarters, branch, or a non-branch outlet; 4 if at headquarters, branches, non-branch outlets, or electronically and 5 if at headquarters, branches, non branch outlets, electronically or over phone. Minimum amount of consumer loan (mortgage) is the smallest amount of loan banks make.

Cost of Transactions (Dimension III)

Fees consumer loans (mortgage) are the fees associated with consumer (mortgage) loans. Annual fees for checking (savings) account are the fees associated with maintaining a checking (savings) account. The costs to transfer funds internationally is the amount of fees banks charge to transfer funds internationally. The amount of fees for using ATM card is the fee banks charge consumers for using the ATM card.

Other dimensions of an inclusive financial system which are not considered in our study, due to non-availability of data are: dimension of gender does the banking system include gender; dimension of access by less privileged people such as disabled and low caste; regional dimension; rural-urban population; access to finance for certain occupations. Within the cost dimension, costs incurred (besides the ones considered in our study) such as the cost involved in travelling to a bank branch, also needs to be taken into account

(World Bank 2008). Due to poor roads and transport access, such costs tend to be high in the poor and less developed areas. Also, rural poor may have to forgo a day's wage to visit bank branches (Singhal and Duggal 2005). In recent years, lack of financial literacy has also been cited as a major reason for financial exclusion, particularly in the developing countries (OECD, World Bank et al. 2009). A number of measures are being taken by different countries to improve financial knowledge of their citizens. There is, however, no indicator to judge financial literacy of people, unlike the literacy rate which is easily available to assess the country's literacy level. Recognising that lack of awareness is a major factor for financial exclusion, the Reserve Bank of India, India's central bank, has lately taken a number of measures to improve financial literacy. In its project titled *Project Financial Literacy* the bank aims to disseminate information on the central bank and general banking concepts to certain groups such as school children, college students, women, rural and urban poor, defence personnel and senior citizens.

Data for the three dimensions as built in our study have been taken from the World Bank database (2007) and CGAP (2009). Data on Afghanistan, Bhutan, and Maldives is not available. Our study focuses mostly on five countries located in the region that is, Bangladesh, Nepal, Pakistan, Sri Lanka, and India, as data on all indicators covered in the study are available for these countries only.

Methodology

Based on UNDP's methodology followed in the construction of HDI, HPI and GDI, Sarma (2008) built a single composite financial inclusion index with values between 0 and 1, where 0 denotes total financial exclusion, and 1 implies total financial inclusion. Sarma (2008) calculated the dimension index for each dimension of financial inclusion that is, banking penetration (BP), availability of non-banking services (BS) and usage of the banking system (BU), by using the following formula:

$$d_i = \frac{A_i - m_i}{M_i - m_i} \qquad \qquad \dots (1)$$

where:

A_i = Actual value of dimension i

m_i = minimum value of dimension i

M_i = maximum value of dimension i

This is broadly in alignment with the methodology used by UNDP in the construction of HDI and other UNDP indices. Sarma points out that higher the value of d_i higher is that country's achievement in that dimension. The differences from the UNDP methodology as Sarma (2008) pointed out, were in respect of adopting a dynamic context of benchmark value rather than a fixed one as adopted by UNDP. For instance, in HDI while computing life expectancy, UNDP takes the fixed maximum value of 85 years and minimum of 25 years for all countries. Similarly the goalposts (maximum and minimum values) for adult literacy rate are 100 per cent (maximum), and 0 at the other end (minimum). Regarding the financial inclusion index (or financial access index in our case) unlike HDI taking a fixed value is not appropriate, and as Sarma (2008) points out "difficult to fix what should be the minimum/maximum for any dimension of financial inclusion." Furthermore, it provides a better picture of the relative index of financial inclusion, and is not a static but a dynamic concept.

In our study, we follow similar reasoning and methodology as in Sarma (2008). Thus for each dimension we have n number of variables:

$$D_i = X_1, X_2, X_3.....X_n \qquad ...(1)$$

For each variable we compute D_i using the following formula:

$$d_i = \frac{A_i - m_i}{M_i - m_i} \qquad ...(2)$$

where:

A_i = Actual value of X_1

m_i = minimum value of X_1

M_i = maximum value of X_1

The minimum and maximum values, termed as 'goalposts' (UNDP, 2009), are the minimum and maximum values of each variable in different countries. For instance, among 98 countries data which was made available in the World Bank database, the minimum number of bank branches geographically per 1000 sq. kilometre was 0.11 in Namibia and Botswana and the maximum number of bank branches was 636.07 in Singapore.

Further, $\quad D_iI = (d_{i1} + d_{i2} + d_{i3}....d_n)/n \qquad ...(3)$

Assigning weights of 2 to outreach, and 1 each to ease and cost of transactions the Financial Access Index (FAI) is derived as follows:

$$FAI = D_iI * w_i / D_iII * w_{ii} + D_i - III * w_{iii} \qquad ...(4)$$

where w_i, w_{ii}, w_{iii} are weights attached to three dimensions that is, outreach, ease and cost of transactions.

As mentioned earlier, we build two indices of Financial Access Index (FAI) which we term as FAI-I and FAI-II. Although, following a similar approach to Sarma (2008) in computing dimensional values, our methodology differs in the way the dimensional indices are combined to arrive at the final index. While Sarma (2008) arrives at the Index of Financial Inclusion (as the study calls it) based on the distance from the ideal, our study takes into account different properties of each dimension in the index. Also, unlike HDI which assigns equal weight to each variable in the index, we assign higher weight to outreach as an easy approach to bank branch, physical or ATM can be regarded as the most important factor in accessing finance.

The data for FAI-I is drawn from the World Bank database on access to financial services (World Bank 2007). These data, however, relate to commercial banks only. As is well known microfinance, cooperative banks, and other financial institutions too are important sources of finance for individuals in South Asia. Our study, therefore, based on CGAP (2009) database builds another series of financial access for the South Asian countries. For the non-banking financial institutions, quantitative data is available only for outreach (branches per 100,000 population) for cooperatives, specialised state financial institutions and microfinance institutions. This is in contrast to FAI-I which was built on three dimensions of financial access that is, outreach, cost and ease of transactions. We term this index as Financial Access Index II (FAI-II).

RESULTS

The results of our study for Financial Access Index (FAI-I) show that India among all the South Asian countries ranks highest, and has the highest level of financial access. This is followed by Sri Lanka, Bangladesh, Pakistan, and Nepal. In Nepal, the ease of using financial system and outreach is very poor. Costs too are high in Nepal (Table 4). Appendix 1 provides in detail the Di values of different variables used in computing Financial Access Index I.

On the proximate reasons why access and usage of finance varies across the countries, per capita income has been found to be an important indicator (Demirguc-Kunt 2010). Our own data plotted in Figure 3 portrays a contrasting picture of some high income East Asian economies, and those in the South Asia region. Thus, the countries in the South Asia region with low incomes per capita have low access to bank branches.

Table 4. Financial Access Index – I

Countries	Outreach (D_iI)	Ease (D_iII)	Cost (D_iIII)	FAI-I	Ranking of Countries in FAI
India	0.024	0.18	0.06	0.063	1
Sri Lanka	0.033	0.17	0.07	0.043	2
Bangladesh	0.029	0.32	0.02	0.028	3
Pakistan	0.016	0.29	0.03	0.015	4
Nepal	0.005	0.63	0.22	0.002	5

Notes:

(i) Outreach has been worked out on the basis four variables; ease of transaction takes 12 indicators into account and cost considers six indicators.

(ii) Outreach is higher as the figure increases; Ease is lesser as the figure increases and higher costs are obviously reflected in higher figures. In Column 5 higher values reflect better financial access and vice versa.

Source: Computed from World Bank (2007).

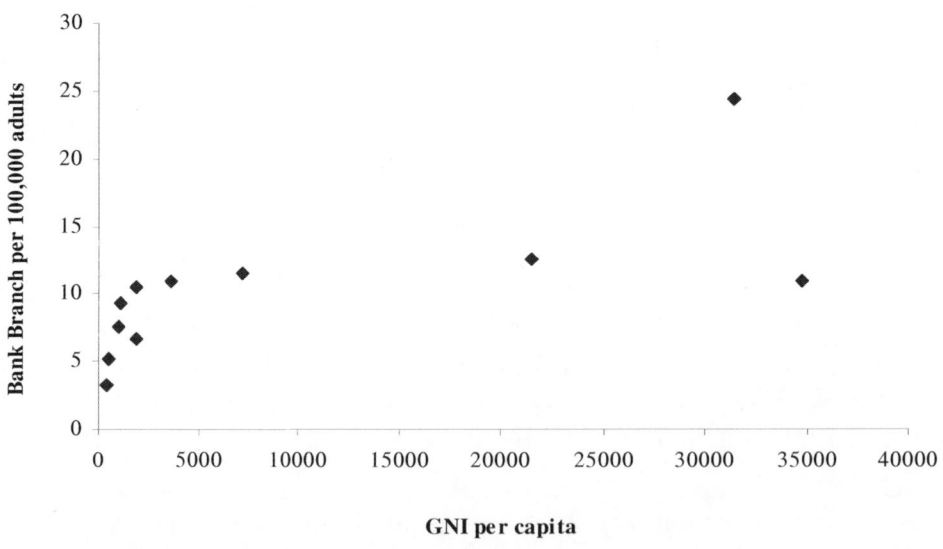

Fig. 3. Economic Development and Bank Branches in South Asia and East Asia

In the Indian context, although government owned banks have been much maligned for their poor and inefficient lending decisions and inefficiencies, yet their achievements in spreading the banking network far and wide, and in improving access has not been much acknowledged. Burgess and Pande (2003) have shown that bank branching in India has led to improvements in income redistribution and poverty reduction.

We also computed Financial Access Index -II covering non-bank financial institutions including microfinance. It may be noted that for no single South Asian country data on all the three non-banking institutions is available. Data for microfinance is not available separately for India as Self Help Groups (SHGs) are linked to the banks.[4] As mentioned earlier, FAI-II includes only outreach dimension due to non-availability of quantitative data for other dimensions, that is, ease of transactions and cost of transactions covered in FAI-I. Thus, in the outreach (branches per 100,000 population) of the non-banking financial institutions Sri Lanka ranks first followed by India. India is followed by Bangladesh, Nepal, and Pakistan. The presence of non-banking financial institutions in Bangladesh is higher than that of Nepal and Pakistan. However, contrary to the common perception of strong presence of microfinance institutions in Bangladesh, the country had only 2.4 branches of microfinance institutions per 100,000 adults (CGAP 2009).

Table 5: Financial Access Index II*

Countries	Cooperatives	State Financial Institutions	Microfinance	FAI- II	Ranking of countries in FAI-II
Sri Lanka	0.654	0.433		0.543	1
India	0.012	0.785		0.398	2
Bangladesh		0.046	0.113	0.079	3
Nepal		0.025	0.089	0.057	4
Pakistan		0.018	0.070	0.044	5

* Includes Di - Outreach of non-financial institutions only. FAI-II is the average of results obtained for three non-banking financial institutions.

The ranking of the countries based on FAI-I and FAI-II is shown in Table 6. As the table shows, except Bangladesh which occupies third place in both the indices, ranking of all other countries in financial access changes in FAI-II. For instance, Sri Lanka is lower to India in FAI-I but ranks above India in FAI-II. Pakistan ranks lowest in FAI-II while Nepal scored higher in the access of finance through non-bank financial institutions.

---

[4] The model of microfinance followed in India is mostly through the SHG-bank linkage programme, wherein the non-governmental organisations which exist for rural development, women, child health etc., and microfinance is one of their activities, form the self-help groups and assist the groups in accessing credit from banks.

Table 6: Ranking of the South Asian Countries in Financial Access Index

Countries	Financial Access Index I	Financial Access Index II
India	1	2
Sri Lanka	2	1
Bangladesh	3	3
Pakistan	4	5
Nepal	5	4

CONCLUSION

The access dimension of finance is gradually being recognised as an important issue in economic development. Emphasis on financial development in the literature and various measures taken up by the policymakers to develop financial system are unproductive, unless finance is accessible to all and barriers to access are removed. In this study, we examined financial access of countries within the South Asia region. This region was chosen as it is fast growing, yet has high levels of poverty and low human capital development.

Despite a growing literature on financial access, a single measure of financial inclusion in different countries does not exist. Our study, therefore, using a multiple indicator and multi-dimensional approach to cover as many dimensions of access as possible, builds financial access index for the South Asian countries. The dimensions covered in our study relate to outreach, ease of transactions and cost of transactions. In contrast to a single indicator in each dimension adopted by Sarma (2008), our study covers as many possible indicators for each dimension, in order to present a more accurate and comprehensive picture of access to finance. Our results show that India ranks highest among all the countries in financial access followed by Sri Lanka and others in the region.

The study is, however, not without its limitations. Although, many possible variables are included in the compilation of index, it still does not take into account rural/urban variables; gender; and people with disabilities, and other costs incurred such as travel costs associated with banking, particularly in the less developed regions and rural areas. Also, as the Financial Access Index has been computed from the survey database, time series data on many of the indicators are not available. The study limits itself to the South Asian countries. The future extensions of this analysis can be to other countries such as building a developed and developing country perspective.

REFERENCES

[1] Beck, T., A. Demirguc-Kunt, et al. (2009). "Access to Financial Services: Measurement, Impact and Policies." *World Bank Research Observer* 24 (1): 119-145.

[2] Burgess, R. and R. Pande (2003). "Do Rural Banks Matter? Evidence from Indian Social Banking" London, London School of Economics.

[3] Caprio, G. and P. Hanohan (2001). "Finance for growth: Policy choices in a Volatile World", Volume 1, Washington DC, World Bank.

[4] CGAP (2009). "Financial Access 2009: Measuring Access to Financial Services around the World". Washington DC, Consultative Group to Assist the Poor/The World Bank.

[5] Chowdhary, O.H. (1991). "Human Development Index: A Critique." *Bangladesh Development Studies* (3): 125-127.

[6] Claessens, S. (2006). "Access to Financial Services: A Review of the Issues and Public Policy Objectives." *World Bank Research Observer* 21 (2): 207-240.

[7] Claessens, S. and E.H.B. Feijen (2007). Financial Sector Development and the Millennium Development Goals". Washington DC, World Bank available at SSRN: http://ssrn.com/abstract=950269.

[8] Collins, S.M. (2007). Chapter 2: Economic Growth in South Asia: A Growth Accounting Perspective. *South Asia: Growth and Regional Integration*, S. Ahmed and E. Ghani. Washington DC, World Bank: 45-60.

[9] De La Torre, A., J.C. Gozzi, et al. (2007). "Financial Development: Maturing and Emerging Policy Issues." *The World Bank Research Observer* 22(1): 67-102.

[10] Demirguc-Kunt, A. (2010). Measuring Access to Finance...One step at a time." Access to Finance, W. Bank. Washington, World Bank. 2010.

[11] Demirguc-Kunt, A. and R. Levine (2008). Finance, "Financial Sector Policies and Long-Run Growth". Washington DC, Commission on Growth and Development, World Bank.

[12] Demirguc-Kunt, A. and R. Levine (2008). "Finance, Financial Sector Policies, and Long-Run Growth." Washington DC, World Bank: 1-82.

[13] Devarajan, S. and I. Nabi (2006). "Economic Growth in South Asia: Promising, Un-equalizing,...Sustainable?" Washington DC 20433, South Asia Region, World Bank.

[14] Fernando, N.A. (2007). Low-Income Households' Access to Financial Services: International Experience, Measures for Improvement, and the Future. Manila, Philippines, Asian Development Bank: 1-36.

[15] Ghani, E. and S. Ahmed (2009)., Accelerating Growth and Job Creation in South Asia" Washington DC, World Bank, Oxford University Press.

[16] IMF (2009). "World Economic Outlook Update: Contractionary Forces Receding But Weak Recovery Ahead". Washington DC, International Monetary Fund (IMF).

[17] King, R.G. and R. Levine (1993). "Finance and Growth: Schumpeter might be right.", *Quarterly Journal of Economics* 108 (3): 717-738.

[18] Levine, R. (1997). "Financial Development and Economic Growth: Views and Agenda," *Journal of Economic Literature* 35 (2): 688-726.

[19] Lewis, W. A. (1955). The "Theory of Economic Growth", George Allen and Unwin.

[20] McGillivray, M. (1991). "The Human Development Index: Yet Another Redundant Composite Development Indicator?" *World Development* 19(10): 1461-1468.

[21] Montenegro, A. (2004). "An Economic Development Index," Retrieved May 17, 2010, from http://129.3.20.41/eps/dev/papers/0404/0404010.pdf.

[22] Nubler, I. (1995). "The Human Development Index revisted," *Intereconomics* 30(4): 171-176.

[23] OECD, World Bank, et al. (2009). "The Case for Financial Literacy in Developing Countries: Promoting Access to Finance by Empowering Consumers" Washington DC, World Bank.

[24] Porter, R. C. (1966). "The Promotion of the Banking Habit and Economic Development" *Journal of Development Studies* 2(4): 346-366.

[25] RBI (2008). Annual Report, 2007-08. Mumbai, Reserve Bank of India.

[26] Sagar, A.D. and A. Najam (1997). "The Human Development Index: A Critical Review." *Ecological Economics* 25(1): 249-264.

[27] Sarma, M. (2008). Index of Financial Inclusion", New Delhi, India, Indian Council for Research on International Economic Relations.

[28] Singhal, A. and B. Duggal (2005). "Extending banking to the poor in India." *Electronic Banking*.

[29] Sophastienphong, K. and A. Kulathunga (2008). "Getting Finance in South Asia 2009: Indicators and Analysis of the Commercial Banking Sector," Washington DC, World Bank.

[30] UNDP (2009). Human Development Report 2009 – Overcoming Barriers: Human Mobility and Development. New York, United Nations Development Programme.

[31] World Bank (2007). "Finance for All? Policy Research Report: Database/Appendix Tables." Retrieved 30 January, 2010, from http://econ.worldbank.org/WBSITE/EXTERNAL/EXTDEC/EXTRESEARCH/0, contentMDK: 21546633~pagePK:64214825~piPK: 64214943~theSitePK: 469382,00.html.

[32] World Bank (2008). "Finance for All? Policies and Pitfalls in Expanding Access", Washington DC, World Bank.

APPENDIX I

Financial Access Index -I

Variable- Di-I	Minimum		Maximum		D_i				
	Country	Value	Country	Value	Bangladesh	India	Nepal	Pakistan	Sri Lanka
Geographic branch penetration (number)	Namibia	0.11	Singapore	636.07	0.07445	0.03532	0.00448	0.01414	0.03192
Demographic branch penetration (number)	Ethiopia	0.41	Spain	95.87	0.04253	0.06170	0.01372	0.04525	0.06767
Geographic ATM penetration (number)	Madagascar	0.07	Singapore	2642.62	0.00020		0.00003	0.00036	0.00410
Demographic ATM penetration (number)	Bangladesh	0.06	Canada	135.23	0.00000		0.00022	0.00348	0.02671
Average					0.029	.049	0.005	0.016	0.033
Variable – Di-II	Minimum		Maximum		Di-II	Maximum		D_i	
Locations to open deposit account (out of 3)		1.00	UK	3.00	0.500	0.500	0.670	0.500	0.400
Minimum amount to open checking account (% of GDPPC)	Spain	0.00	Gabon	141.84	0.016	0.062	0.639	0.011	0.111
Minimum amount to open savings account (% of GDPPC)	Chile	0.00	Gabon	70.92	0.013	0.071	0.894	0.022	0.050
Minimum amount to be maintained in checking account (% of GDPPC)	Belgium	0.00	Nepal	123.77	0.018	0.047	1.000	0.003	0.039
Minimum amount to be maintained in savings account (% of GDPPC)	Belgium	0.00	Nepal	73.83	0.011	0.068	1.000	0.010	0.011
No. of docs. to open checking account (out of 5)	Albania	1.00	Bangladesh	4.57	1.000	0.473	0.871	0.459	0.454
No. of docs to open savings account (out of 5)	Albania	1.00	Zimbabwe	4.72	0.960	0.417	0.785	0.384	0.000
Locations to submit loan applications (out of 5)	Sierra Leone	1.77	UK	5.00	0.108	0.207	0.071	0.409	0.350
Minimum amount consumer loan (% of GDPPC)	Venezuela	0.00	Nepal	1153.17	0.022	0.025	1.000	0.127	0.031

Minimum amount mortgage loan (% of GDPPC)	Venezuela	0.00	Sierra Leone	5157.40	0.274	0.028	0.416	0.185	0.010
Days to process consumer loan applications	Denmark	0.73	Pakistan	20.71	0.436	0.172	0.149	1.000	0.331
Days to process mortgage loan applications		1.00	Chile	70.63	0.466	0.121	0.122	0.394	0.282
Average					0.319	0.183	0.635	0.292	0.172

	Minimum		Maximum		D_i				
Variable – Di-III	*Country*	*Value*	*Country*	*Value*	*Bangladesh*	*India*	*Nepal*	*Pakistan*	*Sri Lanka*
Fees consumer loan (% of min. loan amount)	Japan	0.00	Gabon	109.24	0.002	0.011	0.009	0.001	0.003
Fee mortgage loan (% of min. loan amount)	Switzerland	0.00	Gabon	109.24	0.002	0.007	0.009	0.001	0.017
Annual fees checking account (% of GDPPC)	Bangladesh	0.00	Sierra Leone	26.63	0.000	0.000	0.311	0.000	0.027
Annual fees savings account (% of GDPPC)	Bangladesh	0.00	Zambia	7.79	0.000	0.022	0.638	0.000	0.000
Cost to transfer funds internationally (% of $250)	Belgium	0.12	Chile	20.00	0.091	0.320	0.351	0.100	0.353
Amount of fee for using ATM cards (% of $100)	Argentina	0.00	Dominican Republic	5.70	0.000	0.000	0.000	0.105	0.005
Average					0.016	0.060	0.220	0.034	0.068

Source: Computed from World Bank (2007).

Education for All: An Indian Perspective

K.K. Ganguly

Indian Council of Medical Research (ICMR), New Delhi

ABSTRACT

The policy framework for the development of education and eradication of illiteracy was laid down in the National Policy on Education (NPE) 1986, which had set the goal of expenditure on education at sin pex cent of the GDP. As against this target, the combined total expenditure on education by the central and state governments was 3.74 percent of the GDP in 2003-04 (BE), thus showing lack of commitment on the part of the state to attain the objectives as enshrined in the National Policy on Education 1986. The share of educational expenditure on elementary education was 56 per cent during the First five Year Plan, which came down in the subsequent five years.

EDUCATION FOR ALL 1990

The Universal Declaration of Human Rights, asserted that "everyone has a right to education." Despite notable efforts by countries around the globe to ensure the right to education for all, the scenario is appalling.

More than 100 million children, including at least 60 million girls, had no access to primary schooling till the end of the 1980s, and during this period more than 960 million adults, two-thirds of whom were women, were illiterate, and functional illiteracy is a significant problem in all countries, both industrialized as was a developing.

More than one-third of the world's adults had no access to printed knowledge, new skills and technologies that could improve the quality of their lives and help them shape, and adapt to, social and cultural change.

Besides, more than 100 million children and countless adults did not complete basic education programmes; millions more satisfied only attendance requirements, but did not acquire essential knowledge and skills.

Such a situation warrants serious consultations among the member countries of the United Nation. It was felt that there is urgency to take serious steps towards universal primary education worldwide. Therefore, participants in the *World Conference on Education for All,* assembled in Jomtien, Thailand, from 5 - 9 March, 1990, and a resolution was passed stating:

- Education is a fundamental right for all people, women and men, of all ages, throughout the world;
- Understanding that education can help ensure a safer, healthier, more prosperous and environmentally sound world, while simultaneously contributing to the social, economic, and cultural progress, tolerance, and international cooperation;
- Knowing that education is an indispensable key to, though not a sufficient condition for, personal and social improvement;
- Recognizing that traditional knowledge and indigenous cultural heritage have a value and validity in their own right, and a capacity to both define and promote development;
- Acknowledging that, overall, the current provision of education is seriously deficient and that it must be made more relevant and qualitatively improved, and made universally available;
- Recognizing that sound basic education is fundamental to the strengthening of higher levels of education and of scientific and technological literacy and capacity, and thus for self-reliant development.

India being a signatory to the declaration, embarked on education for all in right earnest. Initiated in the early 1990s, the District Primary Education Program (DPEP) was designed to facilitate India's efforts to achieve universal primary education, and it has since become the world's largest education program, reaching 60 million children.

While the World Bank is the single largest contributor to this initiative, having provided US $1.2 billion, the program was also supported by many other donors, including the European Commission, DFID, UNICEF and the Governments of the Netherlands and Sweden. Spread over 271 districts in 18 states in India, the program operated where female literacy levels are below the national average.

The focus of DPEP were children between the ages of six and 14, and its target was to provide at least four or five years of quality primary education. The project also destined to reduce the number of school dropouts, and improve the overall quality of primary education. In addition to girls who were formerly prevented from attending school, the beneficiaries include children with mild to moderate disabilities, and working children. The programme also had scope and vision to bring tribal, in the fold of compulsory primary education in this country. As a result, enrolment figure enhanced from 38 per cent to 43 per cent in three years time.

The DPEP took the new form of *Sarva Shiksha Abhiyan* as the international donor agencies withdrew from DPEP, but at the same time, the goal of universal primary education was yet to be achieved. The Government of India decided to continue with the programme on its own, and the programme is operational till date.

SARVA SHIKSHA ABHIYAN

The scheme of the Sarva Shiksha Abhiyan (SSA) evolved from the recommendations of the State Education Ministers' Conference held in October 1998, to pursue universal elementary education in a mission mode. The scheme of the Sarava Shiksha Abhiyan was launched by the Government of India in 2001.

Goals of SSA

Goals of SSA are as follows:

- All 6-14 age children in school/EGS centre/bridge course by 2003;
- All 6-14 age children complete five years of primary education by 2007;
- All 6-14 age children complete eight years of schooling by 2010;
- Focus on elementary education of satisfactory quality, with emphasis on education for life;
- Bridge all gender and social category gaps at the primary stage by 2007, and at the elementary education level by 2010;
- Universal retention by 2010.

At a conference of the World Education Forum held in Dakar, Senegal in April 2004, representatives of 164 countries, including India, adopted the Dakar Framework for Action on Education for All. The framework identified six goals, which included:

(i) expanding and improving comprehensive early childhood care and education, especially for the most vulnerable and disadvantaged children;

(ii) ensuring that by 2015 all children, particularly girls, and children in difficult circumstances and those belonging to ethnic minorities, have access to complete free and compulsory primary education of good quality;

(iii) ensuring that the learning needs of all young people and adults are met through equitable access to appropriate learning and life skills programmes;

(iv) achieving a 50 per cent improvement in levels of adult literacy by 2015, especially for women, and equitable access to basic and continuing education for all adults;

(v) eliminating gender disparities in primary and secondary education by 2005, and achieving gender equality in education by 2015, with focus on ensuring girls' full and equal access to, and achievement in basic education of good quality;

(vi) improving all aspects of the quality of education and ensuring excellence of all, so that recognized and measurable learning outcomes are achieved by all, especially in literacy, numeracy and essential life skills.

Probe Study

The Public Report on Basic Education (PROBE) {a survey group from the Delhi School of Economics and some other organizations}, did a country wide evaluation to assess the universal education scenario after India's implementation of the Dakar Declaration. The study found:

Gender disaggregated data on the literacy rate shows that women have stayed behind men in terms of literacy. Literacy rates for men have increased from 24.95 percent in 1951 to 75.85 per cent in 2001. Literacy rates for female have increased from 7.93 per cent in 1951 to 54.16 in 2001. India (61.3 per cent) stands behind China (90.9 per cent) and Sri Lanka (92.1 per cent) in terms of adult literacy. Gross enrolment ratios of girls have stayed below boys in the primary, upper primary and elementary levels of education. However, the enrolment ratio of girls in elementary education has increased from 17.7 per cent in 1950-51 to 79.3 per cent in 2002-03.

Probe also showed various interesting findings after conducting out a study among (BIMARU) states during 1996 in 188 randomly selected villages. By interviewing 1221 households. The study demolished many myths, i.e.

1. Elementary education in India is not free.

   It may well be free, or nearly free, in the restricted sense, that admission fees in government schools are negligible. But, education is not free in the wider and more relevant sense that it involves no expenditure for the parents. The PROBE survey indicates that north Indian parents spend more than Rs. 300 per year (on fees, books, slates, clothes, etc.) to send a child to a government primary school. This is a major financial burden, especially for poor families with several children of school-going age.

2. No Indian parents have very little interest in education.

   The PROBE survey suggests that an overwhelming majority of parents, even those amidst the deprived sections of the population, attach great importance to the education of their children. For instance, 98 per cent of all parents would like their sons to receive at least eight years of education, and even for girls the corresponding proportion is as high as 63 per cent.

3. No economic dependence on child labour is the main reason why poor families are unable to send their children to school.

PRESENT SCENARIO

29 per cent of elementary schools did not have a pucca building in 2009-10, up from 27 percent in 2007-08. Over 49 per cent schools did not have boundary walls, only a slight improvement over two years ago when the proportion was 50 per cent. Girls had a separate toilet in only 59 per cent of schools, again only slightly better than 50 per cent in 2007-08. There is improvement in drinking water and number of classrooms, but the situation is still grim. The net enrollment ratio dropped from about 98 percent in class 5 to 58 per cent   in class 8.

Students in rural areas revealed in its 2010 report that 53 per cent of class 5 students could read a simple text. That's down from 58 per cent in 2007. Only 36 per cent of children could do simple division compared to 42 per cent in 2007. Desperate parents are shifting their kids to private schools where enrollment are up from about 20 percent in 2007 to 24 per cent in 2010. The number of class 8 students taking private tuitions is also up from about 22 per cent in 2007 to 31 per cent in 2010.

Government expenditure – both, state and central combined – on education has grown over the years, from about Rs. 97,375 cr in 2004-05 to Rs. 1,89,325 cr in 2008-09, according to data compiled by the Centre for Budget and Governance Accountability (CBGA). As a share of total government expenditure, the spending on education is stagnating at about 11.6 percent, while as a share of GDP, it has increased only marginally from 3.01 per cent in 2004-05 to 3.4 per cent in 2009-10.

Though the programme seems good on paper, it lacks funds and execution skills, Sustenance and out of box thinking is required to keep the flow of fund steady, in order to get the "Right to Education" implemented in time. The programme also needs mid course assessment (may be every six monthly), to keep it moving like a well oiled machine.

ISSUES THAT NEED TO BE FOCUSED

In this content, one has to begin thinking of better options for teaching tribal children and the minorities, of different religious faiths. They find the curriculum, medium of teaching and examples given by the teacher mostly alien. However, we need to have a curriculum that is more pupil friendly, rather than trying to bring children at par with the rest of the non-tribals. There is however non quick fix solutions, and we have to homogenize them not the reverse. They also should have the option to attend classes as per their convenience and not according to the teachers, otherwise any effort to rope in these children in the main stream will be futile.

A common syllabus over a period of time imparted in a sustained manner will give these children equal opportunities for seeking higher educational or employment opportunities along with the majority.

One of the chronic problems of non attendance in schools is because siblings compromise regular schooling for taking care of siblings, in love there are working parents, mainly in rural India. The *anganwadi* is not yet fully geared up to take care of all preschool children who need serious attention in the absence of their parents or sibs. And preschool children are very intimately affectionate to their family members, that an *anganwadi* worker finds it difficult to care for these children to make them stay put in the *anganwadi*. One of the major goals of universal retention by 2010 has not been achieved so far, and to achieve it, there is need to revamp the programme in a much more holistic and comprehensive manner.

REFERENCES

[1] Ministry of Human Resource Development, Department of Education **Programme Status DPEP**: States. New Delhi, 1997.

[2] Seventh Joint Supervision Mission 14 to 27 March, 1998. Aide Memoire. New Delhi, Educational Consultant India, 1998.

[3] **Srivastava, A B L** Internal efficiency and chorat drop-out rates at primary level of education in Phase IPEP district for 1996-97. New Delhi, Educational Consultants India, 1999.

[4] National Council of Educational Research and Training, Department of Non-**formal Education & Education of SC/ST.** DPEP: Tribal Study Synthesis Report.

[5] India, Ministry of Human Resource Development, Department of Education, DPEP Bureau. Towards participatory planning: a study of the planning process in DPEP based on case studies from the states of Gujarat, Himachal Pradesh, Karnataka, Maharashtra, Tamil Nadu, Uttar Pradesh and West Bengal, New Delhi, 2001.

Interest Free *Microfinance* to Fight Poverty and Unemployment: An Attempt to Explore Possibilities and Challenges in the Indian Context

Habeebul Rahiman[1] and Hasanul Banna[2]

[1]*Department of Social Work, Jamia Millia Islamia, New Delhi*
[2]*Correspondent, Madhyamam Daily, Delhi Bureau*

INTRODUCTION

The present article is an attempt to evaluate the effectiveness of the service delivery of mainstream *micro finance* institutions, identify shortcomings, and to present an interest free co-operative model of *micro finance* as an alternative, which not only overcomes the shortcomings of the mainstream micro finance system, but also functions as a promising tool for addressing massive poverty and unemployment, and boosting human and cooperative feelings among fellow beings in a sustainable manner. It presents case studies of select two organisations that are in pursuit of this innovative model of *micro finance* in the Indian context.

CONCEPTUALISING MICRO FINANCE

Microfinance is the arrangement for providing financial services to the poor, or nearly poor sections of people, as an alternative to the relatively inaccessible mainstream banking services. According to Seibel (2001), microfinance is "a sector of formal and non-formal financial institutions providing micro saving, microcredit and micro insurance services to the micro economy, thereby allocating scarce resources to micro investments with the highest rates of return. In a narrow sense, microfinance institutions are small local financial institutions. In a wider sense, they may also comprise national or regional banks with microfinance services for small savers and borrowers".

Microfinance is considered to be an effective development agent to alleviate poverty. Providing poor entrepreneurs permanent access to an appropriate range of quality financial services, and helping them to come out of poverty has been the main objective of this initiative.

With their objectives in mind, microfinance institutions across the world have been reaching out to a large number of the needy poor. Since the acceptance of microfinance as a tool of financial inclusion and poverty alleviation, several models have been developed for this purpose. The *Grameen Bank Model, Village Bank Model, Credit Unions, Cooperative Societies, Self Help Groups, Commercial Banks, Non Banking Financial Company, Nidhis, Community Banking, Rotating Savings and Credit Associations* have all been experimented with in different parts of the world, primarily to increase the outreach and improve the socioeconomic condition of poor clients.

Microfinance institutions came as a blessing for the financially excluded millions who had no access to the mainstream banking institutes. They did not have access to the services of the very limited branches of mainstream banks in rural areas, due to various reasons, including the issue of providing documentary evidence like identity proof, the inhospitable and un-welcome attitude of the banking staff towards the socially excluded, lack of awareness of poor people regarding the complicated procedures of availing banking services, the requirement of maintaining a high level of minimum balance in the account, and many more such factors.

Despite having the world's largest network of bank branches, India has the world's largest number of people excluded from the financial services network, since over 40 per cent of its population remains included. Lack of access to affordable credit was cited as one of the chief reasons for farmers' suicides by the National Commission on Farmers. It is at this juncture, services of microfinance institutions become relevant and inevitable.

According to the 2009 State of the Sector Report, brought out by Access Development Services and authored by a former NABARD Chief General Manager, N. Srinivasan, micro-finance now reaches roughly 70 million people. Sa-Dhan, the network of MFIs reports that MFRs have reached 234 of the 331 poorest districts in the country, identified by the government. In 2009, the growth of the MFI sector exceeded that of the banking sector, according to the report (Srinivasan, 2009). Until the mid 1990s, MFIs in India functioned as not-for profit NGOs with a public service mission, and worked with rural communities.

COMMERCIALISATION OF MFIs: SHIFT FROM THE PRO-POOR FOCUS

However, in recent times, the credibility of mushrooming microfinance institutions and their *modus operandi* is under a question mark, not only by the 'beneficiaries' and civil society organisations, but by the government itself, who had to step into the scene to regulate their 'service' to the poor for the so called 'financial inclusion', after an uproar over a series of suicides by poor loanees who allegedly resorted to the extreme step due to coercive tactics adopted by micro finance institutions (MFI) for recovery. This and other incidents have led to the mounting criticism of microfinance as a debt trap for the poor.

The large scale commercialisation of MFIs started in the late 1990s. Even the largest commercial MFIs today have their roots in not-for-profit endeavours. *(The SKS Microfinance, India's largest and currently most beleaguered MFI began as Swayam Krusihi Sangham).* Due to commercialisation of MFIs, the strategic focus of microfinance today seems to have shifted from the poor borrowers to profits. The data shows that during 2007-08 Spandana Sphoorthy Financial, the second largest MFI in the country, increased its net profit by 700 per cent. Commercial transformation of MFIS has been accompanied by changes in the structure of ownership, control and management of MFIs and the nature of their stakeholders commitment.

The proponents of commercialisation of MFIs have their own justifications. Inadequate non-commercial sources income to meet the requirements of huge donor capital is one such justification. According to the World Bank estimate, India requires Rs. 2.4 lakh crore for lending to the poor. For this, a for-profit model, with assured return on capital of investors is needed. The high operation cost of MFIs is cited as another justification. MFIs reach out to individuals in remote rural areas by going to them, not by sitting in the nearest big town like mainstream banks. Operation costs and costs of borrowing together make the effective interest rate for an MFI between 22 and 28 per cent. Additionally, they have to even consider a profit margin for their endeavour, which will take the interest rate anywhere between 30-35 per cent and even beyond. Being answerable to their investors, MFIs aggressively pursue their customers for timely repayment with huge interest, using even inhuman tactics, as the individuals unlike firms, cannot be declared bankrupts in India.

Exploring the apparent dilemma of present day microfinance with respect to serving the poor and chasing profits, takes us to the diagnosis that the huge interest rate component involved in the process, which acts as the main culprit, forcing many to end their life and make many more permanently bankrupt.

The basic feature of most MFIs is to provide loans. It has been noted by policy makers that MFIs are making profits by means of the *loan business*. A task force was formed to report on the credit related issues of farmers. This committee was led by the NABARD Chairman, U.C. Sarangi. The Sarangi report says that the new money-lending laws should expand the definition of "moneylender" to include MFIs, since they are closely-held for profit. It also recommends that such MFIs be excluded from priority sector lending benefits, as it is difficult to ascertain if the loans reached those for whom they were meant. (Economic Times, 2010)

The inaccessibility of the real needy to the services of MFIs is another major concern. Present day microfinance institutions are addressing only those who are much above the subsistence level. Even in the case of marginal farmers, only one in every seven has access to credit. The statement that microfinance is alleviating poverty is not wholly correct. The report by Mr. Sarangi notes that "About 38 per cent of loans (to marginal farmers) carry interest rates of 30 per cent or more, while another 36 per cent cost anywhere between 20 per cent and 25 per cent. The implications are predictable – impoverishment, distress, migration and, sometimes, suicide."

Another disturbing report is about the way peer pressure is practiced for loan recovery. Most MFIs, particularly the profit-making organisations, use this tool for recovery which is devoid of any co-relation with the wealth creation process. Most of the MFIs boasted about their performance on the basis of the recovery indicator which, according to them, is more than ninety per cent or above. The recovery should be linked with income. In business, including micro-business, there may be profit as well as loss. The design of recovery should take this fact into consideration. The peer group should come for help when in distress, and if there is a recovery problem due to moral hazard, it should be addressed through motivation, education and legislation. In contrast, the practice of present day commercial MFIs is unethical, inhuman and there is no noble purpose behind the very concept of microfinance.

POSITIONING THE INTEREST FREE FINANCIAL SYSTEM

Discussions on an interest-free financial system should start with a post-mortem of the interest based financial system. The very basis of interest based financial transactions is the profit motive, as it ensures undisrupted flow of profits from the poor to the rich, and needy to the wealthy. The interest based economic system necessitates the existence of the exploiter and the exploited.

The principle of interest based capitalist economic system in plain words, is that every man is the sole owner of his earnings; there are no sharers in his earnings. The ultimate result is disturbance in the equilibrium in the distribution of wealth. It is inherent in this system to create a society which is devoid of compassion and cooperation. The imbalance in the distribution of wealth causes disruption of the blood circulation in the body of the economy. Bulk of the body is destroyed due to circulation deficiency of blood, and the main organs die due to excess accumulation of blood.

Communism on the other hand is based on the principle that all resources of wealth are the collective property of society and as such, an individual would get wages for the services he renders for the common interest of society. It adopts means which are at war against human nature. It ignores the motivating force of personal interest behind human efforts and action. It generates a mega capitalist in the form of the state, by eliminating individual capitalists. This mega capitalist (communist state) does not have any compassion and human sensitivity (Maudoodi, 1946).

To substitute both these views based on the ownership of wealth, a new economic outlook based on the concept of trusteeship of wealth becomes relevant. According to this, the role of human beings as trustees of wealth that is created, and to work in cooperation with each other in the creation of wealth, so as to use it not only for individual benefit, but for the benefit of the entire humanity. Profit should not be the sole motive as per this school of thought. Being a trustee of wealth that is created, he is not supposed to use money as a tool of exploitation, or as a means for harming the social, economic as well as moral healthy coexistence of society. This necessitates prohibition of usury/ payment or acceptance of interest on specific term loans, use of money for gambling, doing business on alcoholic beverages or harmful consumable items.

THE MODUS OPERANDI OF INTEREST-FREE MICROFINANCE INSTITUTIONS

As a way to overcome the evils of the traditional (interest based) microfinance system, a handful of interest-free MFIs have come forward very recently to provide interest-free financial services. The Asian Development Bank (ADB) in its 2006, report points out that "the special characteristics of interest free finance can provide alternative means to reach under served groups in small rural areas and agriculture producers" (ADB, 2006).

Interest free establishments are those institutions which are financing without interest. These institutions finance needy people in different ways, by receiving deposits from the public as shares, and returning it after maturity with a part of profit earned from investments. These institutions provide capital to the unemployed and needy entrepreneurs, and strictly monitor the working of these institutions. Through this, on the one side they create employment, and on the other, and more important side, encourage the productivity of the nation. Providing consumer loans is another important function of interest free establishments.

The working of an interest free institution is based on profit and loss sharing. IFIs receive deposits from people without offering any fixed rate of return. These deposits are invested in various projects handled by the institutions directly, or in the production units run by others. Here we see two types of contracts, institution-depositor contract and institution-entrepreneur contract. The profits earned by the entrepreneur from the invested amount is shared with the institution on a pre-determined proportion. The share of profits received by the financial institution from different entrepreneurs is pooled in a common account, and after meeting the expenditure of the institution, it is shared between the depositors of a pre-determined rate fixed at the time of contract. Instead of interest, the depositor receives a part of the profits.

The literature separates Islamic banking into three main activities: concessional financing, trade financing, and participatory mechanisms. Within these activities, are various contractual forms that conform fully to the tenets of profit and loss sharing. The more commonly used profit and loss sharing transactions are partnership (*mudaraba*) and equity participation (*musharaka*). Lending contracts include benevolent loan (*qard al-hasanah*), mark up sale (*bai'mua'jjal or murabaha*), forward sale (*bai'salam*), leading (*ijara*), and loan with service charge (*Jo'alah*) are some other transactions (Errico and Farahbaksh, 1998). Some of the main instruments used in the interest free microfinance institutions are examined here:

Trustee Partnership (Mudaraba): Trustee partnership is a mode of financing through which the investor or institution provides capital finance for a specific venture indicated by the customer. The investor institution is the owner of the capital, and the customer-entrepreneur is responsible for the management of the business and provides professional, managerial and technical expertise for initiating and operating the business enterprise, or project. Profit is shared according to a pre-agreed ratio.

Joint Venture (Musharaka): A joint venture involves a partnership in which both the bank and its customer-client contribute to entrepreneurship and capital. It is an agreement whereby the customer and the bank agree to combine financial resources to undertake any type of business venture, and agree to manage the same according to the terms of the agreement. Profits are shared between the bank and the customer in a pre-agreed ratio. Losses are shared strictly in proportion to their respective capital contributions.

Cost-plus Sale (Murabaha): Cost plus implies a sale on a cost-plus basis. The mechanism may be described as follows. Individual A is in need of commodity X on debt. He approaches bank B. Now, B buys X from the vendor/ supplier at price P. This price is also known to A. Next, B sells X to A at a marked-up price, say P+M, where M is the agreed profit or mark up taken by B. The payment of price P+M is now deferred to a future date and is made in full or in parts. In *a Murabaha*, both parties to the transaction must know the cost and the profit or mark-up.

Leasing (Ijara): In simple terms, it means leasing or hiring of a physical asset. It is a popular debt-based product in which the interest free bank assumes the role of a leaser, and allows its client to use a particular asset that it owns. The client is in need of the asset. Through leasing, it receives the benefits associated with ownership of the asset against payment of predetermined rentals. Leasing is for a known time period. In cost plus and leasing, the bank is not a natural owner of the asset. It acquires ownership upon receiving a request from its client.

Deferred Delivery Sale (Salam): It is essentially a forward agreement where delivery occurs at a future date in exchange for spot payment of price. Unlike earlier mechanisms, *salam* was originally designed as a financing mechanism for small farmers and traders. Under a *salam* agreement, a trader in need of short-term funds sells merchandise to the bank on a deferred delivery basis. It receives the full price of the merchandise on the spot that serves its financing needs at present. At a pre-agreed future date, it delivers the merchandise to the bank. The bank sells the merchandise in the market at the prevailing price. Since the spot price that the bank pays is pegged lower than the expected future price, the transaction should result in a profit for the bank.

Manufacture-Sale (Istisna): An *Istisna* is a contract of manufacture. A seller under this agreement undertakes to develop or manufacture a commodity with clear specifications for an agreed price, and delivers after an agreed period of time. The unique feature of the manufacturing contract is that nothing is exchanged on the spot, or at the time of contracting. It is pure and perhaps the only forward contract where the obligations of both parties relate to the future. The buyer makes payment of price in parts over the agreed time period, or in full at the end of the time period.

Benevolent Loan (Qard): This is the simplest of all financing schemes. Under this scheme, a borrower in need of a specific amount of funds borrows the same from a lender as *Qard Hasan,* with or without a clear stipulation regarding the maturity date. The loan is repaid on maturity without an increment or interest. When no maturity is stipulated, the loan is repaid when asked by the lender, again without any increment. The lender is allowed to ask for an asset as collateral. The lender is allowed to charge the borrower actual administrative expenses incurred in operation of the mechanism (Palath, 2010).

THE COOPERATIVE MODEL OF INTEREST-FREE MICROFINANCE FOR INDIA

The interest free microfinance system in the Indian context is relatively new, and hence, challenging too. In India, the option of institutionalized interest free finance is available only through two legal routes. One are Non-Banking Financial Companies (NBFC) and another are the Cooperative Credit Societies under liberal acts enacted after 1995 in ten Indian states, and a Central Act for multi state cooperative societies (Ajmal, 2010).

The choice of NBFC route has to face the following issues: (1) at the time of registration of NBFC, an amount of Rupees two crore is required as paid up share capital. (2) NBFC is more suitable for investment rather than microfinance. Those who are practicing microfinance under NBFC complain about the cost of funds.

The Cooperative Credit Society under state and multi state acts is another legal route available for interest free finance, especially microfinance. *Cooperative* embodies the values of self help, mutual responsibility, equality, trust and equity. These values are the foundation stones of the seven universally recognized principles of cooperatives. The Multi-State Cooperative Act provides opportunities to launch interest-free cooperative societies. Statutory compliances under the act are simple and hassle-free. There is no interference in the functioning of the cooperative. A cooperative has the potential to diversify the financial activities encompassing micro-enterprise and micro-insurance on an interest-free basis (Ajmal, 2010).

The 1995 statement of ICA lists seven principles. These principles are part of all ten acts enacted in India after 1995, and also in Multi-State Cooperative Societies Act-2002 (MSCS-2002) as the first schedule. These principles are: (1) Voluntary and open membership; (2) Democratic member control; (3) Member economic participation; (4)

Autonomy and independence; (5) Education, training and information; (6) Cooperation among cooperatives; and (7) Concern for community. The first three principles address the internal dynamics of a cooperative, and the last four affect both the internal operation and the external relationship of cooperatives.

The core philosophical perspective of the cooperative movement is based on "fundamental respect for all human beings" and "belief in their capacity to improve themselves economically and socially through mutual/self-help." The cooperative movement believes that application of democratic procedures in economic activities is feasible, desirable and efficient. It further believes that democratically-elected economic organizations make a contribution to the common good. Hence, cooperative societies are the best fit for starting interest-free micro finance in the Indian context.

INTEREST FREE MICROFINANCE WORLD LEVEL

Interest free micro finance is the part of interest free banks rising in the financial world from the 1970s. Interest free banks are mainly promoted in the Muslim world, because Islam strictly prohibits interest. So interest free banks are also known as Islamic banks.

Interest free banking is viewed as one of the fastest growing segments of the financial service industry. Many studies in different parts of the world, especially in Bangladesh, shows that in a short span of time, interest free MFIs have been performing better than the traditional MFIs in the field of resource mobilization and poverty alleviation (Chowdhury, 2004). Studies also provide ample evidence to show that interest free microfinance is the effective method of poverty alleviation by reaching to the poorest of the poor, than interest based microfinance institutions.

The Banker, a famous finance journal published from the UK explains the growth of the Islamic finance sector in the following words. "Today's Islamic finance industry is growing at a rate of 15 per cent to 20 per cent a year. The Gulf Cooperation Council (GCC) proportion of total Islamic banking assets has reached 30 per cent and is projected to rise to 40 per cent in the next three years. and it is this segment that holds the key to success for the more than 250 Islamic banks that now operate in more than 75 countries worldwide."

Table 1 gives the names of a few world famous interest free institutions in the respective nations.

Table 1: Majon Interest Free Microfinance Institutions in different Couatness

Name of the Institution	Country of Operation
Muslim Aid UK	Srilanka and Indonesia
Hodeidah Microfinance	Yemen
Akhuwath Microfinance	Pakistan
Islamic Rural Banks	Indonesia
Rural Development Programme of Islamic Bank	Bangladesh
Prot Sudan Association for Small Enterprise Development (PASED)	Sudan
Qardhasan Funds	Iran
"Sanadiq" Microfinance Jabal Al Hoss	Syria
Mu'assasat Bayt Al-Mal in Lebanon	Lebanon

Source: Introduction to Interest Free Microfinance by Mohammed Obaidullah IDB Jeddah (2008).

The Question of Being 'Faith Based'

The apprehension of implementing a faith based approach to micro-finance in a secular country like ours is a question to be addressed at this stage. The faith based initiatives for social welfare, though usually started by a group of people, with a particular religious affiliation, need not be stopped from serving the wider public, so long as they adhere to the following principles which are in normal practice in case of interest free micro finance: (a) they do not restrict the benefits of their work to people who share the same faith; (b) they do not depend wholly on funding from members of the same faith, or from funds raised by their institutions, and (c) their staff, even at quite senior levels do not necessarily share the same faith as that on which the agency is based.

As stated earlier, Islam strongly prohibits interest and using money for purposes which are exploitative of social as well as moral health and hence, interest free financing institutions are also known as Islamic banks. According to Islam, money is only a means of medium of exchange. It should be invested in the business, and therefore should not be allowed to give rise to more money via fixed interest. Instead of interest, Islam promotes profit/loss sharing principles. Inculcating ethics or values with financial transactions are the basic feature of interest free Islamic financial institutions. The interest free banking system initiated by the followers of this faith, strongly adheres to these moral values and principles.

It will be quiet relevant to quote here some of the extracts from a recent Kerala High Court judgement on 3 February, 2011 in the case of Dr. Subramaniam Swamy v/s State of Kerala on the matter of Islamic banking initiative. In para 41 of the judgement, the honourable Court observes: *Every legal system has some basis in some religion or religious beliefs. For example, all legal systems known to a civilized world disapproves activities such as theft, causing harm to fellow human beings, licentiousness, etc. and it is also equally true that no major religion known to humanity approves any one of the above activities. Therefore, to categorise laws which disapprove or prohibit such activities as non-secular, merely because the prescription of such laws also coincides with certain religious beliefs and avoid such state action that it should be non-secular, would not be conducive to the promotion of an orderly society either secular or non-secular. If the purposes of the state are to be classified as "non-secular" simply because the mandate of the law made by the state coincided with the beliefs of a religion, or originated in a religion, virtually no law can be made. In our opinion it is for the above mentioned reason both Articles 25 and 26 open with the clause: "subject to public order, morality and health…. .* In para 52 of the same judgement, the Court observes: *If that were to be so, all the policies of the state which provide subsidization of the food to poor people would also attract the prohibition contained in Article 27 as such a practice not only coincides but also is rooted in religious belief common to all major religions that feeding the poor is a meritorious activity.* The Honourable court goes to the extent of saying that : *"The main and primary purpose of the 6th respondent is commerce but propagation of religion. On the other hand, the denial of the state to participate only on the ground that the 6th respondent proposes to carry on the business in compliance with Shariah may amount to discrimination on the basis of religion.*

The Rangarajan Committee suggests: "While interest-free banking is provided in a limited manner through NBFCs and cooperatives, the Committee recommends that measures be taken to permit the delivery of interest-free finance on a larger scale, including through the banking system. This is in consonance with the objectives of inclusion and growth through innovation. The committee believes that it would be possible, through appropriate measures, to create a framework for such products without an adverse systemic risk impact" (Rangarajan, 2008).

CONCLUSION

If on the one hand, the interest based microfinance system failure to deliver the expected duties of serving the marginalized to come out of their vicious circle of poverty, and on the other hand interest free microfinance institutions and banks have displayed their sustainability and robustness in the face of grave financial crises, even when the mainstream banks had to depend on governmental assistance to tide over serious financial problems, it becomes obligatory for a social worker to explore the potential of this emerging system to answer present day crisis of the large mass of poor and marginalized in our country.

REFERENCES

[1] Ajmal, Arshad. (2010), *Interest Free Microfinance in India, Exploring the Cooperative Model Option,* New Delhi: Sahulat Microfinance Society.

[2] Asian Development Bank (2006), 'Aligning the Architecture of Islamic Finance to the Evolving Industry Needs', Keynote address by Haruhika Kuroda, President, ADB, at 3rd *Islamic Financial Services Board Summit* held on 17th May 2006 at Beirut, Lebanon.

[3] Chowdhury, AMR and Bhuiya, A. (2004), 'The Wider Impacts of BRAC Poverty Alleviation Programme in Bangladesh', *Journal oif International Development* 16 (3), pp. 369-386.

[4] Dr. Subrahmaniam Swamy v/s State of Kerala, 3rd February 2011, The High Court of Kerala, WP (C). No 35180 of 2009 (s).

[5] Drrica, Luca and Farah Baksh Mitra (1998), *Islamic Banking: Issues in Prudential Regulations and Supervision,* IMR Working Paper, March, pp. 1-32.

[6] Economic Times (2010), 'SKS Microfinance May Hit Street with Rs 1000 Crore IPO', 15th March, available at http:// economictimes.com/markets/ipos/sks-microfinance-may-hit-street-with-Rs-1000-cror-IPO-/articleshow/5684162.cms

[7] Maudoodi, Abul A'la Sayed (1946), *Sood,* New Delhi: MMI Publisher.

[8] Obaidullah and Khan, Tariqullah (2008), *Interest Free Microfinance Development; Challenges and Initiatives',* Jeddah: Islamic Research and Training Institute

[9] Palath, Mohammed (2010), *Interest Free Micro Finance in Different Countries,* New Delhi: Vision 2016.

[10] Rangarajan (2008), 'Broadening Access to Finance', *The Rangarajan Report,* Chapt -3.

[11] Sibel, HD (2001), 'Mainstreaming Informal Financial Institutions', *Journal of Developmental Entrepreneurship,* Vol. 6, No.1, April: 83-91.

[12] Srinivasan, N. (2009), *State of the Sector Report,* Access Development Services, as quoted in Srinivasan, Rukhmini, (2010), 'Scam of Small Things', *Times of India Crest,* Nov, 2010.

Case Study 1: *Alkhair Cooperative Credit Society, Patna, Bihar*

Alkhair Cooperative Credit Society was registered under the Multi-State Cooperative Societies Act, 2002. It has the permission of the Central Registrar to operate in four states: Bihar, Jharkhand, Uttar Pradesh, and Delhi. Presently, there are three branches of the Society at Phulwarisharif, Patna and Arrah. Process is underway to establish branches in Jharkhand and Delhi states. Nature of the microfinance institution was actually decided within the broader framework of economic justice, equity and cooperation.

Al-Khair is functioning with a clear stand on the following issues:1) Interest is strictly forbidden. 2) Service charge should not exceed the actual operational cost. 3) Service charge is neither interest nor has it to become a source of profit. 4) Micro-credit should primarily be based on micro-savings without external funding. 5) No physical collateral is to be demanded for micro-credit. 6) Call deposit is not to be blocked for a single day. 7) Ample loanable funds can be created by dint of cycling of micro-deposits, withdrawal and repayment   of   loans. 8) Charity and loans are not to be mixed up. Loan is to be given after assessing loanable worth. 9) Time default in refund of loan is to be expected among poor people, but payment default is rare, and even that under unusual situations. 10) Micro-credit on interest-free basis is sustainable and can play an effective role in poverty alleviation.

The following are the main objectives of *Al-Khair*: Socio-economic development of the marginalized section of the society, Promotion of micro-savings, self-help activity and cooperative values among members, Expansion of microfinance activities on interest-free basis, encouraging micro-enterprise on a profit-loss share basis, providing micro-insurance safeguard to micro-entrepreneurs on *takaful* basis.

Loans are granted to members only. Eligibility for loans is decided on the basis of the deposit profile of a person and credit limit is equal to ten times his share value. Loanable worth is decided on the basis of his deposit behaviour. Loan may be granted up to 100 times of his daily deposit with credit limit. *Al-Khair* has developed following products of loans in consonance with the basic principles of Islamic financing:1) Demand loan, 2) Marked up loan, 3) Short term business loan.

Al-Khair has developed following products of deposits in consonance with basic principles of Islamic finance: 1) Call deposits (include daily deposit, monthly deposit and special daily deposit), 2) Time deposits (these are actually fixed deposits without any interest thereon. There are two time deposit instruments, i.e. Sahyog Fund (Cooperation) and earmarked fund, 3) Amanat account, 4) Hajj account, child account and social welfare fund.

Illustration of Short Term Business Loan (STBL or Mudhariba Loan) Model

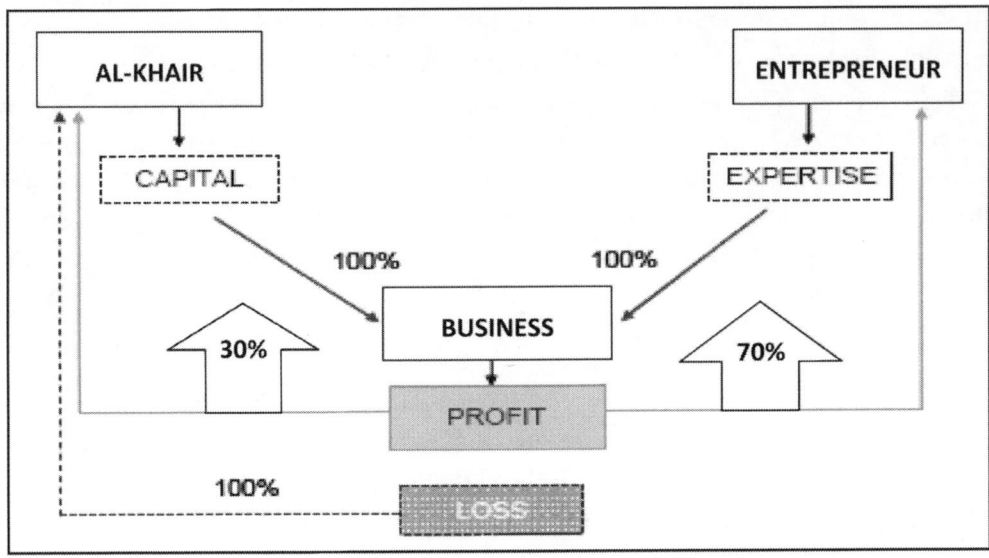

Illustration of Cost plus finance *(Murabiha Loan)*

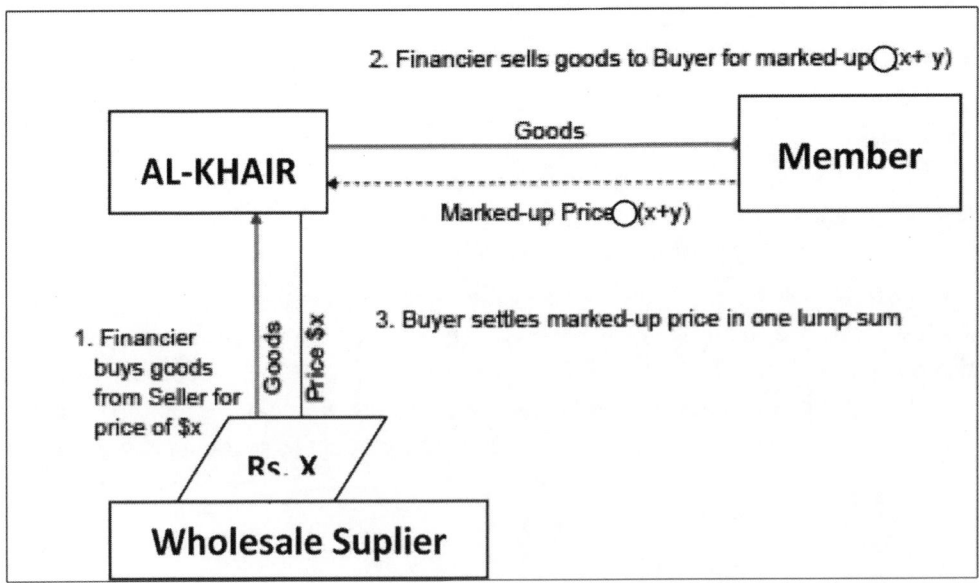

Case Study 2: *Sahulat Microfinance Institution, New Delhi*

Sahulat Microfinance Society is a relatively new but ambitious society set up to establish, facilitate, train, promote and advocate for the establishment of interest free microfinance institutions all over the country. Sahulat Microfinance Society was formed after several meetings and discussions among 21 eminent scholars, economists, professionals and social activists drawn from across the country. Sahulat came into existence as a registered society under the Societies Registration Act of XXI of 1860 on 23 September, 2010. It is a voluntary, non-political, non-profit making social service organisation to provide interest-free micro-finance options for removing socio-economic disparities, and to achieve justice and equity for educationally and financially backward sections of the public at large.

SAHULAT aims at: 1)Facilitating, promoting and developing interest-free micro-finance institutions (IFMFI), 2) Undertaking and promoting need based research and developing different products and financial instruments for IFMFI, 3) Establishing training institutes and data banks for IFMFI and evolving an internal check system and audit facilities and coordination with affiliated institutions, and 4) Advocating with policy makers for a justifiable national policy on interest-free micro-finance in India.

The society shall be a facilitating and promoting agency for launching interest-free microfinance cooperative movement all over the country. The target for the next five years is to establish at least 500 microfinance units in different places all over the country. For each branch of the cooperative, Rs. 6 lacs is required as seed money, to meet the establishment costs and to start the interest-free credit activities in the targeted localities. As per their financial projection, a cooperative branch would become self-reliant in 3 to 5 years time. These branches would succeed in mobilizing the daily-earning families for micro-savings, and daily depositing the amount in the local cooperative branch. Thus, once a cooperative branch is started, local people are involved in the interest-free cooperative activities generating huge amounts, from the micro-deposits from the low income group. The micro-deposits so generated are utilized for interest-free credit to cooperative members by maintaining liquidity requirements. Through these branches, it is expected that 77 lakhs families shall avail the interest-free loan facility for small business and other productive needs.

SMFS objectives are aimed at fighting against the socio-economic disparities in society irrespective of caste, creed or religion, through interest-free microfinance institutions which are proposed to be started at 500 places all over the country. Sahulat shall also mobilise other agencies for convergence of educational, health, housing, self-employment and moral awakening activities in the target areas of interest-free cooperatives, towards achieving the goal of poverty alleviation. Training, survey, research and development are other broader areas under operation at SMFS.

Flow Chart Showing the Products of Sahulat Microfinance Society

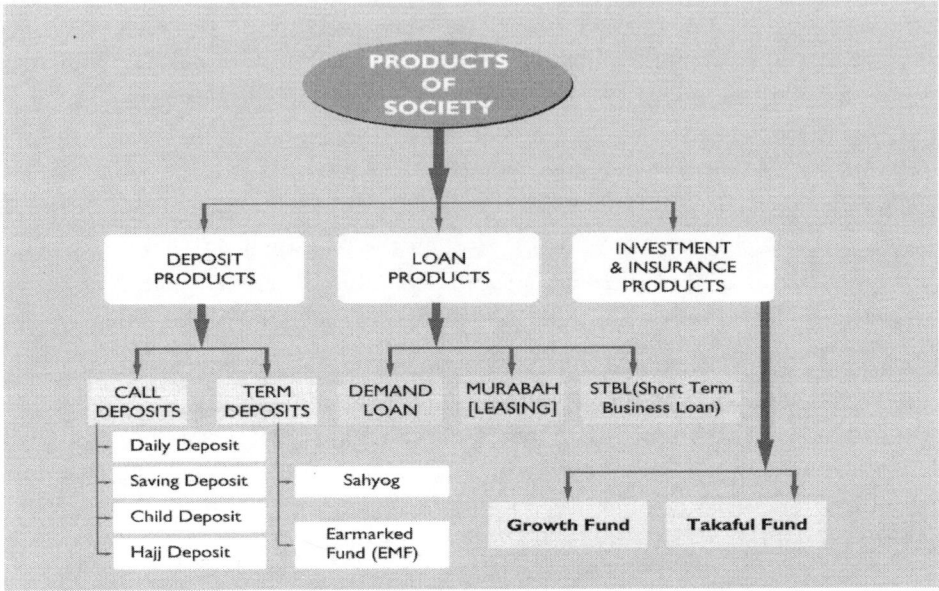

Flow Chart Showing the Modus Operandi of Sahulat Microfinance Society

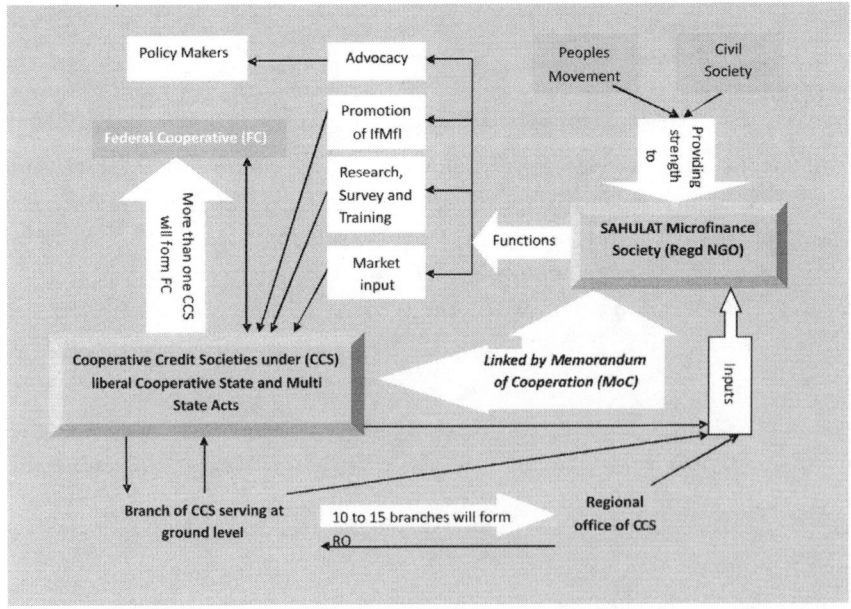

New Education Policy and Social Exclusion Among Dalit Children

V.B. Saharey

Department of Social Work, Jamia Millia Islamia, New Delhi

ABSTRACT

The Dalits (Scheduled Castes) in a caste structure were historically excluded from knowledge and education in traditional Hindu society. Schools were therefore legally opened to these communities in the mid nineteenth century. However, attempts by Dalits to avail education were met with considerable opposition from the upper castes (Nambissan, 1996). At the time of India's Independence in 1947, Dalits had a significantly lower literacy and school enrolment rates, as compared to the rest of the population. In the post Independence period, constitutional provisions, policy thrusts in education as well as parental aspirations for the education of their children brought an increasing proportion of Dalit children into schools. However at the close of the last century, it was found that barely 48 per cent of Dalit children had completed primary schooling (IIPS, 2000). Even today, the vast majority of Dalit children 'drop-out' from school well before they complete eight years of education. The present article analyses how the social exclusion/ discrimination is still prevalent in terms of education in India. It also highlights the extent of social exclusion despite enforcement of various education policies by the state and Right to Education Act, 2009. The article attempts to bring into focus the necessity of a critical examination of the currently ongoing "structural educational adjustment and reform." It deals as to what extent and in what ways do the oppressive and unjust hierarchies of the caste system continue to 'lock' Dalit children out of full participation in education within schools. The article concludes by arguing that in order for social policy to adequately respond to social exclusion in primary education in India, a holistic approach should be adopted including addressing the structural and basic causes of the problem in a context-specific, comprehensive manner.

INTRODUCTION

Indian society has lived a millennium in the system of caste-feudal patriarchy, where education is limited to same sections of society. Education is one of the most important factors affecting the development of children. It has great intrinsic significance as access to education is an important right (Article 28, Convention of the Rights of Children), and being educated is an important and very valuable capability. In addition, getting educated is an important participatory process for children, and equal access for all to this process allows participation in, and respect by society. In fact, many of the early calls for mass education in the 18th and 19th centuries viewed the inclusionary nature of the education process, and the fostering of citizenship through education as more important, than the skills one may acquire through education (Rothschild, 1998).

The post-Independence Constitution perceived education as a crucial parameter to bring about drastic changes. It was seen as the key instrument for bringing about a social order based on value of equality and social justice. Expansion and democratisation of the education system was sought, the two primary egalitarian goals of which were the universalisation of elementary education and the educational "upliftment" of disadvantaged groups. Education is one of the important means of reducing ignorance and inequality in society. It helps an individual to raise one's social status in various ways. Knowledge, skills, values, and attitudes acquired through education help one to lead the desired quality of life. Knowledge and education must be made available to all. As Dr. B.R. Ambedkar, chief architect of the Indian Constitution said, "In the complex world man lives at his peril and he must find his way in it without losing his freedom. There can, under these circumstances, be no freedom that is worthwhile unless the mind is trained to use its freedom. Deprive a man of knowledge and you will make him inevitably the slave of those more fortunate than himself. De-privation of knowledge is denial of the power to use liberty for great ends. An ignorant man may be free but he cannot employ his freedom so as to give him assurance of happiness" (Ambedkar, 1947).

Although Gandhi, Tagore and Krishnamurti (all from the high castes) received national attention as educational philosophers and have been applauded for their contributions to education in India, but education did not incorporate the anti-caste-patriarchy and anti-hegemonic discourses of Phule, Ambedkar, and Periyar. Phule perceived education as a potent weapon in the struggle for revolutionary social transformation. For him, the purpose and content of education was radically different from both Brahmanical and colonial models of education. His ideal was an education that would bring awareness among the socially excluded lower castes of oppressive social relations, and their hegemonic moral and belief systems that pervaded their consciousness (O'Hanlon, 1985; Velaskar, 1998). Like Phule,

B.R. Ambedkar defined the purpose of education in terms of mental awakening and creation of a social and moral conscience. Education was also the means of overcoming an inferior status and state of mind, of wrestling power from the powerful. Thus, the Ambedkarian agenda for education included development of capacities and qualities necessary for entry and leadership in modern avenues of work and politics, and inculcation of self-respect and aspirations to respectable lifestyles in which demeaning traditional practices would have no place (Velaskar, 1998).

As per the 2001 census, Dalits make up 17 per cent of the total population and consistently fare poorly across various indicators related to primary education. Historically, they have faced restrictions in attaining education which is reflected in low literacy rates and levels of education. Empirical evidence indicates that children from the SCs social group suffer from exclusion and discrimination in terms of education. Although the Right to Education Act 2009 and the 83rd Constitutional Amendment recognizes education as a fundamental right of all Indian citizens, disparities continue to be pronounced between the SCs and general castes. Moreover, the Government of India has a provision in the Constitution, which contains explicit state obligation towards protecting and promoting social, economic, political and cultural rights. "The State shall promote with special care the educational and economic interests of the weaker sections of the people and, in particular, of the Scheduled Castes and shall protect them from social injustice and all forms of exploitation" (Directive Principle of State Policy, Article 46). Article 15(4) underscores the state's basic commitment to positive discrimination and Article 21A provides for free and compulsory education to all children in the 6-14 years age-group.

EDUCATION POLICIES AND EDUCATION LEVELS AMONG DALITS

After Independence, the Government of India took a number of steps to strengthen the educational base of persons belonging to the Scheduled Castes. Pursuant to the National Policy on Education 1986, and the Programme of Action (POA) 1992, the special provisions for SCs have been incorporated in the Departments of Elementary Education and Literacy and Secondary and Higher Education. The relaxed norms for opening of primary/middle schools; a primary school within one km walking distance from habitations of population up to 200, instead of habitations of up to 300 population. One of the six basic principles of the National Common Minimum Programme (NCMP) of the United Progressive Alliance (UPA) government states its intention "to provide for full equality of opportunity, particularly in education and employment for Scheduled Castes, Scheduled Tribes, OBCs and religious minorities." The Ministry of Human Resource Development states: "the nation is firmly committed to providing Education for All, the priority areas being free and compulsory primary education, covering children with special needs, eradication of illiteracy, vocationalization, education for women's equality, and special focus on the education of SCs/STs and the Minorities" (Annual Report, 2005-06, HRD, GOI). Abolition of tuition fee in all states in government schools at least up to the upper primary level. The proactive provisions for Dalits comprise of access to free education, free supply of text books and uniforms, scholarships and reservations, meant to compensate for the long history of prohibition and exclusion from education. Reducing the gap between Dalits and other social groups and providing level playing fields and equal opportunities are the stated objectives of many of these programmes.

Also a number of educational programmes have been introduced by the government such as Sarva Shiksha Abhiyan (SSA), a historic stride towards achieving the long cherished goal of Universalisation of Elementary Education (UEE), District Primary Education Programme (DPEP). Similarly, the National Programme for Education of Girls at the Elementary Level (NPEGEL) started under the existing scheme of Sarva Shiksha Abhiyan (SSA) provides additional components for education of girls who are underprivileged/ disadvantaged at the elementary level.

In 2000, literacy rates among the male and female SCs was 52 and 24 per cent respectively compared to 76 and 48 per cent among the general social group. The level of education among the SCs is also lower as compared to the general group. For instance, in 2000, among the SCs the proportion of illiterate and literates up to the primary level together constituted 73 per cent, and only one-third of them possess education beyond the middle school level. Further, only 15 per cent of the SCs were educated up to the middle level, while this proportion was higher (21 per cent) for the general (NSS 55th Round, 1999-2000). Similarly, as we go up the education ladder, at each level, the percentage of educated among the SCs is lower as compared to the non-SCs. Additionally, it is also observed that the disparity between SCs and others in the educational background is the highest at the higher levels of education. Despite various educational programmes and policies with regard to Dalits, educational exclusion and discrimination exists in multiple ways among them.

SOCIAL EXCLUSION AND EDUCATION

As a definition: "social exclusion reflects the multiple and overlapping nature of the disadvantages experienced by certain groups and categories of the population, with social identity as the central axis of their exclusion" (Kabeer). Amartya Sen draws attention to various meanings and dimensions of the concept of social exclusion, and this distinction is drawn between the situations where some people are kept out, and where some people are being included. He described the two situations as 'unfavourable exclusion' and 'unfavourable inclusion' (Sen, 2000). The 'unfavourable inclusion' with unequal treatment may carry the same adverse effects as 'unfavourable exclusion.' The concept of social exclusion essentially refers to the processes through which groups are wholly or partially excluded from full participation in society in which they live (Thorat, 2007). The term exclusion emphasizes very strongly on social factors concerns such as housing, health, employment and education. It excludes certain communities and groups from interaction and access to social resources through social arrangements, normative value systems and customs. It revolves around societal interventions and institutions that exclude, discriminate, isolate and deprive some groups on the basis of group identities like caste and ethnicity. Scheduled caste people, previously referred to as the "untouchables" and "socially excluded," have been historically excluded from formal education due to their oppression under the caste feudal society and subsequent marginalisation by the dominant society. For the scheduled castes who have sought education as a mechanism to transform as well as enter "mainstream" society, the central questions are of representation of their knowledge and culture, and value systems of their lived reality and of social relationships based on dominance and exclusion. In the context of 'education and social exclusion' means a denial of full participation in any kind of learning activities, which may be caused by caste and ethnicity or lack of financial means.

SCHOOL ATTENDANCE AND DROP-OUT RATE OF DALITS

Various studies indicate a wide gap between Dalits and non-Dalits with regard to school attendance. At the aggregated level in 2000, 70 per cent of children in the age group of 5-14 were enrolled in schools in rural India. The data from the Ministry of Human Resources Development, Government of India shows a steady increase in the enrolment rate of Dalit children over the years. The provisional enrolment ratio in 2004-2005 was 98.8 per cent an increase of 18 percentage points from 1989-90 which stood at 80.8 per cent. The enrolment ratio of Dalit children in primary schools during 2004-05 was 115.38. However, with the rising enrolment is the persistent problem of drop-outs (Ministry of HRD, GOI). The school drop-out rate is relatively high (5.2 per cent) among the SCs and the proportion of children who have never attended school (36 per cent) is also relatively higher (NSS 55th Round, 1999-2000). In 2004-2005, 31.47 per cent from among the 98.8 per cent of Dalit children enrolled in Class 1 dropped out by Class V. The drop-out rate reached 52.32 per cent by Class VIII and 62.69 per cent by Class X. 8.17 per cent Dalit children (numbering 3,104,866) in the 6-14 age groups were estimated to be out of school compared to 3.73 per cent of non-SC/ST/OBC children (numbering 1,848,378).

With respect to the general category, it clearly indicates that the school attendance rate is the highest (78 per cent) for this social group as compared to the SCs in 2000. As a result, the drop-out rate is also lower (four per cent) among them as compared to the SCs. The third National Family Health Survey (NFHS), 2005-06 indicates that the SC population is disadvantaged when compared to other castes. Just 21 percent of SC children have completed primary education compared to 70 percent of children belonging to other castes. Further analysis shows that only 64 per cent SC children age 5-18 years were attending school compared to 72 per cent of other caste groups and 22 per cent of SC children have never attended school compared to only 16 percent of children from other castes.

A comparison of the data across social groups clearly indicates that the general category has the highest school attendance rates, and the lowest drop-out rates as compared to the SCs. Conversely, the SCs segment has the highest drop-out rates and the lowest enrolment ratio as compared to the OBCs and the general group. The SCs also have the highest proportion of children who have never attended school. Side by side with increasing enrolments, is also the persistent problem of out of school children and the widening inequalities between Dalit and general social groups in education, both in number and in quality. A relatively high drop-out rate and non-enrolment among the SCs indicates that 'economic deprivation and poor social conditions coupled with inadequate support from the government and agencies at the school level has created extremely unfavourable conditions for children from these sections of society to continue studies at the school level (Thorat, 1999).

SOCIO-ECONOMIC STATUS AND SCHOOL ATTENDANCE

The inter-linkage between economic deprivation and poverty and non-attendance/drop-out ratio is more directly confirmed. It shows the distribution of children attending school, drop-outs and never attended by Monthly Per Capita Expenditure class (MPCE) in rural areas. It reveals that with an increase in the MPCE class from Rs. 225 to Rs. 950 and above, the proportion of those attending school rises from 65 per cent to 92 per cent, and the proportion of those never attended school declined quite systematically from 30 per cent to 5 per cent. Among the relatively lower MPCE classes, the drop-out rate as well as the proportion of children who never attended school were generally of a high order. In fact, little less than 60 per cent of the total drop-outs in rural areas come from the MPCE category of less than Rs. 340, which also happens to be the range closer to the poverty line limit of Rs. 327 MPCE in 1999-2000(NSS 55th Round 1999-2000).

With respect to the comparative analysis across social groups, the ratio of drop-outs among those living below the poverty line is higher (60 per cent) for SCs, as compared to their counter parts from the non-SCs/STs social group (37 per cent). Similarly, the proportion of children who have never attended school living below the poverty line is higher for the SCs, as compared to their counterparts from the non-SCs. The overall pattern, thus, is of higher drop-out and non-attendance rates for the Dalits, as compared to non-Dalits with the gap being especially wide in the lower MPCE categories. There are various empirical evidence of the exclusion that Dalit children face, as a higher proportion of these children drop-out or never attend school, as compared to children of non-Dalits from similar economic backgrounds, i.e. poor and agricultural labour households (NSS 55th Round, 1999-2000).

A further search for the reasons for not attending school, shows that 87 per cent of the children in rural areas indicated non-economic reasons, such as meeting labour shortages, in the household, acquiring skills, lack of school facilities, meeting own expenses for not currently attending school etc. On the other hand, only 13 per cent of the children reported economic reason, i.e. lack of affordability as the main cause for not attending school. Across social groups, as well non-economic reasons were stated to be more important for non-attendance in schools. Deprivation from primary education in SC children was also examined by their households' economic status. NFHS-3 has defined economic status of households by taking household assets and housing characteristics. The analysis indicates that completion of primary education among SC children is lower in all categories of economic status, compared to other castes children. There is hypothesis that drop-out from school is generally high for SC children than other caste children, the study finds the same.

ACCESS TO SCHOOLS

Poor accessibility of schools is one of the important factors for low literacy among Dalits. By 1997, India had as many as 598,000 primary and 177,000 upper primary schools. However, easy access schooling has always been relatively poorer for the Dalits, as compared to the population in general, especially in rural areas. A study by the National Council of Educational Research and Training (NCERT) reveals that schooling is available within a significantly smaller number of predominantly Dalit habitations 37.03 per cent as compared to general rural habitations (49.79 percent). With regard to upper primary schools, access within Dalit habitations is lower (6.51 per cent) as compared to general rural habitations 13.87 per cent (NCERT, 1998).

Very few studies on social accessibility of schools are available. Aruna (1999) in her study of Tamil Nadu, a south Indian state, refers to "qualitative dangers" to schools and says that "in many habitations, the school is situated in localities inhabited by upper castes who are hostile to students belonging to the lower castes and minority groups." Ramaiah's observations of a village, Akramesi, in Tamil Nadu where Dalits form a small minority, have disturbing implications for social accessibility of schools. None of the scheduled castes were allowed to walk through the residential areas of dominant castes, or through the village's main street running through the residential areas of the dominant castes. They had to walk a long way along the periphery of the village to reach their huts (Nambissan and Sedwal, 2002).

According to the Sixth All India Educational Survey conducted by NCERT (1998), Dalit communities mainly avail government schooling. Of the Dalit children in primary schools, 91.3 per cent in rural areas and 64.6 per cent in urban areas were in schools managed by the state government and local bodies (municipalities or corporations). Many of these schools are plagued by various problems, such as lack of basic infrastructure, classrooms, teachers, and teaching aids. Dilapidated buildings, leaking roofs and mud floors appear quite common in schools and provide a depressing atmosphere for children. Teaching aids, apart from black-boards, are relatively absent. The conditions of the schools can be quite appalling, as seen in this description of a school for Dalit girls: "the environment of this institution was reported to be very dirty as the ground was swampy and there were cow-dung heaps and firewood stocked all over."[4] There is also the problem of absenteeism of students and teachers, etc. Thus Dalit children do not have access to quality education. They also face discrimination and discouragement from higher caste community members, who perceive education for Dalits as both a waste and a threat. Their hostility to-wards Dalits' education is linked to the percep-tion that Dalits are not meant to be educated, are incapable of being educated, or if educated, would pose a threat to village hierarchies and power relations (Vasavi et al., 1997).

Another study by (PRIA, 2010) undertook an action learning research to explore the factors and processes affecting the educational processes of Dalit children in three districts of Bihar, viz. Vaishali, Madhubani and Rohtas. Data on households, community and schooling issues were gathered covering 40 schools to examine the trends of social exclusion among Dalit children in the state. As many as 58.5 per cent of schools situated in Dalit habitations do not have separate toilets for girls, village education committees were not formed in 42.5 per cent of the schools, very low attendance of Dalit children, availability of Dalit teachers in only 17 per cent of the surveyed schools, and irregular supply of teaching learning material in 50 per cent of the schools situated in Dalit habitations. Mostly

Dalit children are physically punished even for small mistakes, which develops a sense of fear about schooling and teachers in them.

SEGREGATION IN SCHOOLS

Dalit children's right to education free from discrimination is constantly undermined by the treatment they receive in school. Teachers maintain and impart discriminatory attitudes in their classrooms, forcing children to sit in the back of the room, segregating Dalit children from non-Dalits during lunchtime, forbidding non-Dalit children from sitting next to Dalit children or touching their plates, expressly limiting Dalit students participation in class, subjecting them to verbal abuse and grading them unjustifiably low marks. Sometimes, their teachers often subject Dalit children to corporal punishment. Instances of Dalit students being made to sit/eat separately, their copies/slates not being touched by higher caste teachers, and children themselves not being touched are commonly reported. Like Dalit students, even Dalit teachers are segregated from non-Dalit teachers in accessing food and water during lunchtime. Discrimination against Dalit teachers at times turns violent. In December 2005, members of the dominant caste who could not accept the fact that their children were being taught by a Dalit assaulted Satyanarayan Prasad, a Dalit teacher, in a village in Bihar. When the teacher attempted to lodge a complaint with the police, the police termed the incident as "insignificant" (CHR & GJ and HRW, 2007). Biased attitudes of high caste teachers towards Dalit students are well documented. As the UN Special Rapporteur on the right to education noted in his report before the 67th session of the then-Commission on Human Rights, "teachers have been known to declare that Dalit pupils 'cannot learn unless they are beaten' (E/CN.4/ 2006, Paras). Noted journalist, Sainath, reported that in Rajasthan, one of the twenty eight states of India, children of the Balmiki (traditionally scavengers) caste, seen as most polluting of castes, "are made to sit on their own mats, often outside the room or at the door" (Nambissan and Sedwal, 2002).

Another study documented some of the discriminatory practices against Dalit children in schools of Uttar Pradesh, such as discrimination against Dalit settlements in the location of schools; teachers refusing to touch Dalit children; children from particular castes being special targets of verbal abuse and physical punishment by the teachers, and low caste children frequently being beaten by higher caste classmates (Derez and Gazdar 1996). Studies also suggest that the formation of peer groups is influenced by the caste status of children, and friendships are formed mainly within the boundaries of caste membership. In one of the government schools that Rekha Kaul studied, children complained that though prejudices and discrimination were not practised very openly in the classroom, and the peer group appeared friendly in school, outside the school attitudes changed. Children of upper castes did not invite the Kuruba or Dalit children home for playing, and there was no social intermixing outside the school (Kaul, 2001).

POOR PHYSICAL INFRASTRUCTURE OF SCHOOLS

A majority of studies suggest that physical/infrastructural facilities are totally inadequate and particularly deplorable in schools accessed by Dalits. As mentioned earlier, the majority of Dalit children are in regular government schools. Buildings are dilapidated or badly in need of repair, and basic furniture and teaching equipment is non-existent or of pathetic quality. There are of course state and regional variations. The poorest of physical infrastructure and basic amenities afflict schools in remote areas. There is also a high incidence of very poorly and irregularly functioning schools. The reports from rural Punjab, Orissa, and Rajasthan's Dalits dominated districts reveal shortages of basics such as classrooms, drinking water facilities and teachers. Reports of neglect, indifference, greater teacher absenteeism from Dalit dominated schools have accumulated, pointing to the grim reality that exists on the ground. Exceptions too have been noted, for example studies of Garhwal, Himachal Pradesh, Gujarat, Maharashtra and Kerala show that there are several regions in which the SC have a fairly good provision for education. In certain areas in Maharashtra for, e.g. Zilla Parishad schools are fairly good (Berntsen, 1990).[1] Further, it is important to break the common misconception that rural schools are necessarily worse than urban. There are indications from Maharashtra that government rural schools may be in far better shape than urban municipal schools. This is so because most rural schools have a mix of higher and lower castes/classes, whereas in urban areas where the choice of schools is greater, the municipal schools cater almost exclusively to the poor, lower castes[2].

INADEQUACY OF TEACHERS AND TEACHING TRANSACTIONS

A highly inadequate teaching force has been the most critical element of unequal provisioning. Teacher-pupil ratios in schools frequented by SC have been much higher than those in other schools meant for higher caste villagers. Multi-grade teaching often amounts to very limited teaching or no teaching at all. The problem of insufficient number

---

[1] K. Sujatha (1994, 2000); Kingdon (1996); Thakur (1997); Nambissan (1997, 2000, 2002); Probe (1999); Govinda (2002); Jha and Jhingran (2002). For a useful survey of literature on the quality of education in various parts of the country see Bhatty (1998).

[2] The state of urban schools is reported in studies surveyed in Bhatty (1998); see also Banerji (1997, 2000); Berntsen (1990); Wankhede (1998).

of teachers has been compounded by the problem of unmotivated teachers, which is reflected in the phenomenon of teacher, absenteeism. Teachers for SC children primarily belong to non-SC or non tribal backgrounds. They are highly irregular in attending since they live outside the villages. This is a common feature in schools located in remote areas. There are reports of 'paper schools' which remain closed during the year, and yet others for years on end especially in remote areas. A study of education conducted in eighteen villages from seven states showed that teacher absenteeism was rampant in SC areas of Orissa and Madhya Pradesh. It was common for teachers to mark fictitious attendance of children (Jha & Jhingran, 2002). In the Education Grantee Scheme (EGS) schools in the SC dominated district of Madhya Pradesh multi grade teaching was generalised. The quantity of teaching was problematically low and quality was equally a key deficiency (Leclercq, 2003).

In the school and in classrooms, teacher-pupil interaction is central to teaching and learning processes. Teacher's social background (caste, religion, language), affect their interactions with students. Middle class higher caste teachers are very unhappy with the environments of schools for the poor, and are poorly motivated to teach children of the poor, particularly of SC backgrounds, who are 'derogatorily' categorised as uneducable. Many evidence suggests teacher's preconceptions, bias and behaviour, subtle or overt, conscious or unconscious, operate to discriminate against children of SC backgrounds. Teachers are observed to have low expectations from SC children and girls, and a condescending and downright abusive attitude towards poor children from slums. Teachers also have stated or unstated assumptions of "deprived" and "deficient" cultural backgrounds, languages and inherent intellectual deficiencies of SC children. They follow discriminatory pedagogic practices of labelling, classifying and teaching styles, and operate on the basis of "realistic" perceptions of low caste children's limited cognitive capacities and life chances. For example teachers beliefs about Mushar children in Bihar are that they are just not interested in education, and that they do not have any 'tension' in life (Kumar, 2004). Such presumptions set effective and in the teachers' view legitimate limits to their teaching efforts. Levels of hostility and indifference to Dalit/tribal cultural traits and value systems are high. Discriminatory behaviour manifests itself in numerous ways. Teachers perceive Dalit children in a negative light, see them as unclean, dishonest, lazy, ill-mannered etc. The children could be criticized for their clothes, the dialect they speak, the dislike of uncouth habits of meat eating and alcohol consumption, the ignorance of their parents and even the colour of their skin! They are punished and shouted at, in efforts to discipline and "civilize" them!

Several studies have shown that SC children do not encounter practices related to untouchability in schools (Jodhka, 2000, 2002; Shah, 2000 PRIA, 2010). However, others point to varied forms of direct and subtle discrimination. For instance, Artis et al. (2003) found that in village schools of Gujarat, SC children are forced to sit at the back, actively discouraged to participate in class, are subject to food and water taboos. Similar experiences exist for village schools in Karnataka (Eddie Premdas, personal account). In relation to Dalits, teachers refuse to correct their notebooks and complaints to headmasters results in beating of children. Indeed teacher violence against Dalit children throughout the country is widely reported.

Like the Dalit children, teachers also suffer humiliation and discrimination (Jha and Jhingran, 2002; Heredia, 1992; Samavesh, 2003; Jodhka, 2000, 2002). They are largely isolated or compelled to form their own separate social circles. They also find themselves succumbing to dominant religion-cultural practices in a bid to avoid conflict and gain acceptance (Chaudhary, personal account). A disturbing tendency noted by several studies, and further substantiated by poignant personal narratives is the use of children as servants by high caste teachers. Children are assigned a range of menial tasks from cleaning and sweeping the school to fetching '*paan*' and cigarettes for the teacher (Artis et al, 2003; Talib, 1998, 2000; Sachidananda, 1989). They assign SC children menial jobs and shift the onus of low learning on children and their families. There is an undue obsession with language purity and correctness (Saxena and Mahendroo, 1993; Kundu, 1990, 1994). Placing disadvantaged students in 'better quality' schools doesn't seem to solve the problem. Studies have suggested that feelings of isolation, alienation and experiences of discrimination do neutralize the impact of better facilities.

There are a few studies that have broadly pointed to the role of caste in education, for instance in discriminatory teacher attitudes, denigration of Dalit students, assigning them menial tasks in school as well as caste based peer relations (Balagopal and Subrahmanian, 2003; Nambissan, 2006). Discrimination by teachers towards Dalit children is commonly found in many schools. Teachers have been found to maintain discriminatory attitudes and practices that underlie caste relations in society. B.K. Anitha's study in Karnataka revealed that Dalit pupils were called *Kadu-jana* (forest people) who would not learn without being beaten (Anitha 2000). Anitha's research on classroom processes in Tumkur district of Karnataka also found that the school day was significantly shorter in schools in the Dalit concentrated villages, as compared to the other schools studied. This was mainly because: "a majority of these teachers do not stay in the village and belong to the dominant castes, displaying a distinctive negative attitude towards the education of children of low castes" (Anitha, 2000). Jabbi and Rajyalakshmi, in their study in Rajasthan found that fear of teachers and corporal punishment are factors that parents (especially of Dalit children) cite as constraining regular school attendance (Jabbi and Rajyalakshmi 2001). Kancha Illaiah (1996) refers to his own teachers of higher castes in school who always used to say that: "if he was a Brahmin he hated us and told us to our faces that it was because of the evil time because of *kaliyuga*, that he was being forced to teach 'Sudras' like us." However there is little research that identifies spheres and processes of exclusion and discriminatory practices in school, and how they influence Dalit children's experiences of education. The roots of educational deprivation of Dalit communities must be traced back to their position as untouchables in the caste structure of traditional Hindu society.

PROBLEMS AND PERSPECTIVES

Sixty four years after Independence the situation has improved marginally. Low literacy rates for Dalits are a clear indication of the ways in which the school system fails Dalit children. The last two decades have spelt the decline of the welfare state under the powerful impact of global economic forces and neo-liberal economic policies. The egalitarian ethic underlying change and development is being rapidly decimated. The ideology of the Indian state's New Economic Policy emphasizes the pre-eminence of markets and profits. In the context of an elite directed consensus on the inevitability of liberalisation and structural adjustment, the predominant problems and debates of education have undergone major shifts. Structural adjustments have provided the legitimacy and impetus for a number of educational reforms that pose a direct threat to the mission of universalising elementary education, and equalising educational opportunity for Dalits, especially those left behind. The state is withdrawing from social sectors of education and health, and delegating its social commitments and responsibilities to private agencies and non-governmental organisations. There is already enough indication that basic educational needs of the Dalits are getting seriously undermined under the new dispensation, adversely affecting life chances of vast sections of those who have yet to make the shift to first generation learning. But educational inequality and exclusion, particularly of Dalit children, is a stark social reality across the country, due to their oppression under caste feudal society and the latter their spatial isolation, cultural difference and subsequent marginalisation by the dominant society. Unequal schooling has limited the educational opportunities of disadvantaged Dalit children in India.

To what extent do the oppressive and unjust hierarchies of the caste system continue to 'lock' Dalit children out of full participation in education, and in what ways does this happen within schools? This is an issue that has surprisingly been neglected by the education policy, pedagogic discourse as well as research. However, there is little research that identifies spheres and processes of exclusion and discriminatory practices in schools and how they influence Dalit children's experiences of education.

The low education level among the SCs affects their capacity to participate in better economic activities and make them ineligible to avail regular salaried jobs. This in turn leads to the disadvantaged status in society. The causes of the disadvantaged status related to education of children from scheduled castes are largely unaddressed, and therefore are significant barriers to attending school. Furthermore, the structural causes of social exclusion, such as continued high levels of poverty of scheduled caste children, also remain as significant constraints. However, the gap between upper and lower castes children with respect to completion of primary education is still persisting, due to various socio-economic factors. Discrimination and exclusion of marginalized groups are issues that are increasingly receiving the attention of social scientists of late. This is now widely accepted that developments in state and society in post independent India have not conformed to the expectations, as discrimination and exclusion still persists in our society. Disparities among social groups have also been the result of particular forms of discrimination and exclusion prevalent in society. Discrimination and exclusion marginalizes certain groups from full participation in the social, economic, political, educational and cultural life of the country.

Indeed, so to say that educational institutions are seen as the critical platform for change becomes the medium and the very apparatus to insinuate humiliation and discrimination at the inception of caste identity. In other words, discriminatory practices have been internalized by the higher caste groups towards the Dalit *(teacher, colleague, student, peer groups)* in education and social networking on an every day basis. More strikingly, education has not been significant to perpetuate awareness against, nor ensured a value system that can resist discrimination at the grassroots level.

Deliberations and discussions during the sharing centered on the processes of social exclusion of Dalit children and suggested variables for framing an inclusive educational policy. Issues such as status of residential schools for Dalit children, sensitivity of teachers towards Dalit children, infrastructure in schools located in Dalit habitations, scholarships for Dalit children, and quality of education were raised. Several suggestions were made for ensuring equitable access to education among Dalit children like free education, adequate numbers of residential schools, effective implementation of schemes and provisions, and implementation of RTE in its true spirit. There is also an urgent need for change in the mindsets of policy makers and implementers.

REFERENCES

[1] Ambedkar, B.R. (1987). *Writings and Speeches*, Vol. 3. Mumbai: Government of Maharashtra.

[2] Anitha, B.K. (2000) *Village, Caste and Education*. New Delhi/ Jaipur, Rawat Publications.

[3] Annual Report, (2005-06). Dept. of Elementary Education and Literacy, Dept. of Secondary and Higher Education, Minatory of Human Resources Development, Government of India.

[4] Aruna, R. (1999). "Learn Thoroughly: Primary School-ing in Tamil Nadu", *Economic and Political Weekly*, 1 May, 1011-114.

[5] Balagopalan, Sarada (2003) *Neither Suited for the Home nor for the Fields: Inclusion, Formal Schooling and the Adivasi Child*, in Subrahmanian, Ramya & others (eds.) *Education Inclusion and Exclusion: Indian and South African Perspectives, IDS Bulletin*, Vol. 34, No. 1, January, Sussex: Institute of Development Studies, pp. 55-62.

[6] Census 2001, Government of India.

[7] Dalit Children in Rural India issues related to Exclusion and Deprivation, working Paper Series, Volume III Number 05, 2009, Indian Institute of Dalit Studies.

[8] Derez, Jean and Haris Gazdar. (1996). "Uttar Pradesh: The burden of Inertia", in Derez Jean and Amartya Sen, editors, *India Development*, Oxford University Press. New Delhi

[9] Illaiah, Kancha. (1996). *Why I am not a Hindu*. Samya Publications, Calcutta.

[10] Jabbi, Mona and C.Rajyalakshmi. 2001. "Education of Marginalised Social Groups in Bihar", in Vaidyana-than, A. And P.R. Gopinath Nair, editors, *Elementary Education in Rural India: A Grassroots View*. Sage Publications, New Delhi.

[11] Jha, Jyotsna & Jhingran, Dhir (2002). Elementary Education for the Poorest and Other Deprived Groups: The Real Challenge of Universalisation, New Delhi: Centre for Policy Research.

[12] Jodhka, Surinder S. (2002) "Caste and Untouchability in Rural Punjab", *Economic and Political Weekly*, Vol. XXXVII No. 19, pp. 1813-1257.

[13] Kaul, Rekha (2001). "Accessing Primary Education: Go-ing Beyond the Classroom," *Economic and Political Weekly*, 13-19 January, 36(2).

[14] Kothari, Miloon (2006), Economic and Social Council E/CN.4/2006/41, Commission on Human Rights Sixty-second session Item 10 of the provisional agenda Economic, Social and Cultural Rights.

[15] Kumar, Ravi (2004) "Educational Deprivation of the Marginalised – The Case of Mushar Community in Bihar", Paper presented at Seminar on *Towards Quality Education for All: Issues and Challenges Beyond 86th Amendment at India International Centre*, New Delhi, Council for Social Development, New Delhi.

[16] Leclercq, Francois (2003) (a) "EGS and Primary Schooling in Madhya Pradesh", *Economic and Political Weekly*, Vol. XXXVIII No. 19, pp. 1855-1869.

[17] Nambissan, Geeta B. (2000). "Dealing with depriva-tion", Seminar, No. 493.

[18] Nambissan, Geetha B. and Mona Sedwal. (2002). "Edu-cation for All-The Situation of Dalit Children in India", in Govinda, R., editors. *India Education Report, A Profile of Basic Education*. Oxford University Press, New Delhi.

[19] National Council of Educational Research and Training. 1998/1999. *Sixth All India Educational Survey*. NCERT, New Delhi.

[20] National Sample Survey (1999-2000): Employment and Unemployment Situation among Social Groups in India, 55th Round, NSSO, New Delhi.

[21] Report of Social and Rural Research Institute, 2006.

[22] Rothschild, Emma. (1998). Adam Smith on Education and Instruction. Centre for History and Economics Working Paper. Cambridge: King's College.

[23] Sen, Amartya, (1999). *Development as Freedom*, New York.

[24] Shah Ghanshyam (2000) Hope and Despair: A Study of Untouchability and Atrocities in Gujarat, in Beteille, Andre (ed.), *Journal of Indian School of Political Economy*, Vol. XII, Nos. 3 & 4, pp. 459-472.

[25] Sinha S. (2005), "Reaching out to Undernourished Children: Social Inequalities and Policy Perspective," *Journal of Health and Development*, Vol 1, No. 3-4, Oct-Dec 2005.

[26] Thorat, S.K. & Sadana, Nidhi (2004), "Magnitude, Determinants, and Activities of Child Labour in Rural India", in G.K. Lieten, R. Srivastava & S. K. Thorat (eds), *Small Hands in South Asia, Child Labour in Perspective*, Manohar Publishers & Distributors, New Delhi.

[27] Vasai, A.R. and P.G.Chand, Vijaya Sherry and R. Shailesh Shukla (1997). "Blueprint for Rural Primary Education: How Viable?", *Economic and Political Weekly*, December.

[28] Velaskar, Padma (1998) Ideology, Education and the Political Struggle for Liberation: Change and Challenge Among the Dalits of Maharashtra, in Sureshchandra Shukla and Rekha Kaul (eds), *Education, Development and Underdevelopment* Sage Publications, New Delhi.

Author Index